Barbara K. Given

Teaching
to the Brain's
Natural
Learning Systems

Association for Supervision and Curriculum Development
Alexandria, Virginia USA

Association for Supervision and Curriculum Development
1703 N. Beauregard St. • Alexandria, VA 22311-1714 USA
Telephone: 1-800-933-2723 or 703-578-9600 • Fax: 703-575-5400
Web site: http://www.ascd.org • E-mail: member@ascd.org

All Web links in this book are correct as of the publication date below but may have become inactive or otherwise modified since that time. If you notice a deactivated or changed link, please e-mail books@ascd.org with the words "Link Update" in the subject line. In your message, please specify the Web link, the book title, and the page number on which the link appears.

Printed in the United States of America.

May 2002 member book (p). ASCD Premium, Comprehensive, and Regular members periodically receive ASCD books as part of their membership benefits. No. FY02-07.

ASCD Product No. 101075
ASCD member price: $19.95 nonmember price: $23.95

Library of Congress Cataloging-in-Publication Data
Given, Barbara K., 1935-
  Teaching to the brain's natural learning systems / Barbara K. Given.
    p. cm.
Includes bibliographical references (p.   ) and index.
  ISBN 0-87120-569-6 (alk. paper)
  1. Learning, Psychology of. 2. Brain. I. Title.
  LB1060 .G555 2002
  370.15'23--dc21
                                      2002001331

ISBN: 0-87120-569-6

11 10 09 08 07 06 05 04 03 02   10 9 8 7 6 5 4 3 2 1

Teaching to the Brain's *Natural* Learning Systems

Acknowledgments

For reading the manuscript and offering splendid advice regarding the neuro-biological aspects of the brain's five major learning systems, I extend heartfelt appreciation to Robert Sylwester and Harold Morowitz. To all those who have guided me along my never-ending journey toward translating the neuroscience literature for educational application,—especially colleagues at the Krasnow Institute for Advanced Study—I extend a special thank you.

I extend a special thank you to Teresa Zutter, Director of Alternative Education Programs in Fairfax County Public Schools, for her ongoing support and friendship. For manuscript suggestions along the way, a heartfelt thank you to Claudia Kilmer, Molly Minor, and especially John O'Neil. A loving thank you is sent to my children, Bryce and Bethany, for their unflagging support through the years, and to my major cheerleader, Al Doby.

Introduction

Emerging scientific insights into how the human brain functions are creating considerable excitement for educators; however, the process of translating findings from neuroscience into educational application has been spotty, at best. The purpose of this book is to discuss the brain's natural learning systems as a neurobiological framework for educational practice, based on how the brain learns.

Chapter 1 presents the brain as a complex of five major learning systems—emotional, social, cognitive, physical, and reflective—and explains the linkages between these systems and the mind's basic psychological needs to be, to belong, to know, to do, and to experiment and explore. Chapters 2–6 discuss each of these learning systems in some depth, in terms of their structures, functions, driving forces, and behavior patterns that produce the following outcomes in students:

> *Passion* for learning.
> *Vision* for seeing what is possible.
> *Intention* for developing knowledge and skills.
> *Action* for transforming dreams into realities.
> *Reflection* for self-monitoring and staying the course.

Along the way, I highlight teaching roles and behaviors associated with each system to show how teachers can *inhibit* or *facilitate* passion, vision, intention, action, and reflection in classroom settings. Chapter 7 explores the simultaneous functioning of all five systems as if they were "theaters of the mind" (Baars, 1997; Damasio, 2000a; Given, 2000a).

Throughout the book, I share various ways of applying neuroscience to education, because I believe that unless educators—and policymakers—build bridges between these two disciplines, children and society will be the losers. Education is more than reaching certain standards of learning; education is developing a desire to learn, knowing how to learn, and implementing teaching practices based on how the brain actually functions.

If children are to learn to their fullest and if they are to benefit themselves and society, we must honor their own individual learning systems. As Hamer and Copeland (1998) advise in *Living with Our Genes: Why They Matter More Than You Think:*

> Giving children love and knowledge is as essential as giving them food, but at some point, parents [and teachers] must understand that children are already on a path beyond anyone's choosing. Children are who they are, and parents [as well as teachers] are better off getting to know their own children than trying to mold them into some ideal created out of thin air. Children are to be discovered as well as shaped; they should be allowed and encouraged to develop to their own potential. . . . Each of us is born into the world as someone; we spend the rest of our lives trying to find out who. (p. 25)

A major role of educators is to know enough about brain research to help students develop into the best *who* they can possibly be. As educators, we can rely on the five major neurobiological learning systems to construct a well-organized educational framework that makes lesson planning exhilarating and implementing our plans exciting.

1

The Brain's Natural Learning Systems

undreds, maybe thousands of books about the brain have been published during the past 12 to 15 years, probably more than in the many decades before. Without question, educators want to learn as much as possible about how the brain functions in the limited time available to them for personal study. After all, teachers are responsible for what happens to somewhere around 20 to 150 young brains every school day. Even so, one might ask, "Do educators really need to understand how the brain functions to be effective teachers?" Probably not, because some teachers naturally stimulate and sustain the enjoyment of learning in youngsters. A teacher can have a storehouse of information about brain functioning and remain ineffective. Nonetheless, even the most successful teacher can use an introductory knowledge of how the brain functions to answer perplexing questions about why specific teaching techniques either work or do not.

In *Multimind: A New Way of Looking at Human Behavior*, Robert Ornstein (1986) describes different ways of learning as the brain's natural operating systems. He is not talking about different intelligences, which are advanced by Howard Gardner (1983) in *Frames of Mind*. Rather, Ornstein, a psychologist and neurobiologist, approaches the brain as a biological organ of multisystems related to brain structures:

> Stuck side by side, inside the skin, inside the skull, are several special-purpose, separate, and specific small minds . . . . The particular collection of talents, abilities, and capacities that each person possesses depends partly on birth and partly on experience. Our illusion is that each of us is

somehow unified, with a single coherent purpose and action. Others present a smooth, seemingly consistent and unified surface as well. But it *is* an illusion, as we are hidden from ourselves, just as the skin covers a lot of different organs that are only visible once the covering has been lifted . . . . We are not a single person. We are many . . . . All of these general components of the mind can act independently of each other, they may well have different priorities. (pp. 8–9)

Ornstein goes on to discuss human "multiminds" from several perspectives. He likens each individual to a crowd of people who act unconsciously and automatically, often without the willful direction or consent of all its members. He describes diverse control centers and different kinds of memories associated with each "mind." According to Ornstein, "Some people [in the crowd] are good at learning by rote; some have a good memory for names, some for people, some for places; some people remember conversations; others forget errands and chores; some can retrieve the right bit of information at the right time. These are all fairly separate mental abilities, and different people have their own combination of them" (p. 22).

Ornstein is not alone in his description of multiple minds. Psychiatrist Richard Restak (1991, 1994), author of two Public Broadcasting Service series and several influential texts on the brain, advances the concept of brain "modules"—interconnected collections and columns of neurons that reach across six neuronal layers in the brain cortex and into all parts of the organ to reciprocally exert their power of influence. I earlier wrote about systems of interconnected modules as "theaters of the mind" (Given, 2000), and Baars (1997) calls brain modules "theaters of consciousness." At one moment, an emotional "movie" may demand attention while the cognitive system struggles to make sense of new learning. At other times, hunger or illness may force consideration of the physical movie as systems wax and wane in their influence.

Left and Right Brain Functioning

Multimind/modular-brain thinking is a fairly new concept that grew unexpectedly from split-brain research in the 1960s. At that time, Joseph Bogen, Roger Sperry, and their doctoral students Michael Gazzaniga and Joseph LeDoux used a 1940s technique to control epileptic seizures in patients whose medication was unsuccessful (Gazzaniga, 1985). In several epileptic patients, they cut fibers that connect the two brain hemispheres—called the corpus callosum—and found that the seizures disappeared (Gazzaniga, 1985). Not only that, the researchers were surprised to learn that the right and left sides of the brain behave in uniquely discrete ways. They discovered that the right hemisphere is dominant for visual-constructional tasks and some—but not all—emotion. Later, Damasio (1994) and his colleagues found supporting evidence that the two hemispheres are asymmetrical in how they process emotion. Interestingly, the split-brain research launched exploratory mergers between neuroscience and education. Until split-brain research, education traditionally focused on language and logical thinking.

Jerre Levy and Sperry then defined hemispheric differences by stating that the right brain specialized in holistic processes and the left in analytical processes (Gazzaniga, 1985). After preliminary results were published in the early 1970s, the field was awash with excitement about how the two hemispheres control different mental processes. Their reports prompted many teachers to "teach to the neglected right brain" (for example, see Edwards, 1979). Even though there seemed to be no overt ill effects for patients after split-brain surgery, Michael Gazzaniga (1985), a biologist and researcher in the effects of surgical interventions, believes that separating the two hemispheres created covert or hidden differences; he designed a series of experiments to evaluate subtle changes previously undetected. Additional surprises began to emerge. Gazzaniga found that in some people, either half-brain could respond to visual input and drawing tasks. He demonstrated that the right brain could accurately execute written commands and that language interpretation was in the right as well as the left hemisphere. Based on this research, Gazzaniga and his colleague Joseph LeDoux concluded that all brains are *not* organized in the same "right-brain/left-brain" way.

What was initially overlooked but later found to be critically important was that location—left or right hemisphere—mattered less than the specific brain systems used to handle specific tasks (Gazzaniga, 1985). In other words, specific brain systems function in *either* or *both* hemispheres but depend on the circumstances of the brain's overall growth and development. For example, language is usually a left-brain function, but it may be primarily located in the right hemisphere for people whose left hemisphere fails to support its development. Efforts to downplay hemispheric global versus analytic differences fell on virtually deaf ears. The early misinterpretation, however, was not a total disaster. Some educators made dramatic changes, such as deliberately including visual-spatial (e.g., drawing) and physically active tasks within lessons that were traditionally restricted to linguistic or mathe-matical mental processes.

Current knowledge, however, has moved beyond the left/right dichotomy to a broader view of five different learning systems—emotional, social, cognitive, phys-ical, and reflective—and their numerous, often overlapping subsystems that reflect specific neurobiological brain structures and functions.

The Brain's Basic Operating Systems

Billions of brain cells or neurons construct modules and subsystems that operate synergistically in patterned ways to create five major learning systems. That is, neu-rons organize themselves within modules, systems, and subsystems with incredible precision as if they were diligently filling specific "job descriptions" within a major corporation. The process begins with rapid cell development in utero.

Marian Diamond, neurobiologist and author of *Enriching Heredity* (1988) and *Magic Trees of the Mind* (Diamond & Hopson, 1998), reports that neurons develop at the surprising rate of 50,000 to 100,000 per second during embryonic develop-ment. Calculate the number of seconds in nine months, and the amount of neurons becomes incomprehensible. Obviously, neurons are incredibly tiny; more than 70,000 can jam into a space no bigger than the head of a pin (Kotulak, 1996). As the brain develops before birth and during the first year of life, neurons migrate to their genetically determined location. During this time, about half the brain cells die (Diamond & Hopson), apparently because their developmental work is complete or they simply are not needed.

Eventually, each neuron loosely connects with other neurons by way of tiny spaces called synapses, which are located between the ends of one neuron (axon terminal) and the beginning of another neuron (dendrites and cell membranes). Neurons are like shy teenagers who reach out to hold hands but fail to actually touch one another. Nonetheless, neurons connect loosely at incredible speeds, and, like fickle lovers, they change their connections rapidly. In fact, the University of Chicago's Peter Huttenlocher (Kotulak, 1996) finds that connections often form at the rate of three billion a second, and Diamond and Hopson (1998) note that some single neurons make an astonishing 200,000 connections at any one time. Even more surprising, scientists now believe it is the activity occurring in those tiny spaces that produces consciousness, rather than within the neurons themselves as previously believed.

As incredible as neurons are, they cannot do all the mental work alone. Each neuron is supported by *glial cells*, which carry nourishment to the neurons. Erik Ullian (2001) and his neurobiology associates at Stanford University School of Medicine found that glial cells are necessary for synaptic action. They state that "few synapses form in the absence of glial cells and . . . the few synapses that do form are functionally immature" (p. 569). They also discovered through extensive imaging, immunostaining, and electron microscopy that "glial [cells] may actively participate in synaptic plasticity," or, how synapses change in their function (p. 569).

Together, neurons and glial cells assemble themselves into clusters and layers called modules and circuits. *Modules* are clusters of neurons that huddle together like family members in a hurricane. Adventurous neurons reach outside the family cluster to "talk" with neurons in other modules, and this communication process creates *circuits*. Like telephone wires connecting communities, neuronal connections between cortical regions form networks of neurons that converse on a regular basis. A network that processes similar input is called a *system*, and systems link with other systems to form intricate networks of larger systems at progressively higher levels of complexity (Damasio, 1994; Restak, 1994). In this way, various modules link to one another and form multiple neuronal pathways that, in turn, form cortical regions or communities.

Gerald Edelman (1992), recipient of the Nobel Prize for Physiology in 1972, calls these processes of cell migration into various modules and circuits the "theory of neuronal group selection." Each module or circuit has a specialized genetic design that makes it an expert in one arena of interaction with the world. Some circuits process various emotions, some social interactions, some sensory information, whereas others deal with thinking or pertain to movement, to color, and so forth. Because these complex systems process information in specialized ways, they may be called *learning systems*. Learning systems are guided by the genetic code, but—and this is where educators come into the process—they are subject to environmental input for their detailed formation of response patterns or behaviors. *Thus, teachers have an important role to play in how the learning systems of individual children develop.*

The key to the development of learning systems is the interplay between the hard-wired, genetic aspects of who we are and the soft-wiring added by all kinds of experiences. Without question, parents and teachers have considerable influence over the soft wiring. As Hamer and Copeland (1998) discussed in their book on the science of personality, this relationship is not an either/or proposition; it is nature *and* nurture. They emphasize that "it's part of our nature to respond to nurture" (p. 24). The learning line between nature (genetics) and nurture (available learning opportunities) is a porous one, with one flowing into the other. The resulting mix of nearly equal proportions (Panksepp, 1998) creates a fantastic opportunity for teachers whose instructional behaviors make an incredible difference in how children's learning systems develop and function.

My purpose is to develop a depth of understanding about the primary learning systems—emotional, social, cognitive, physical, and reflective—and then demonstrate how teachers can use these learning systems to meet or surpass local and national learning standards. I believe that when teachers understand how the brain's major learning systems function, they will teach more effectively while gaining more joy in teaching.

Learning Systems Framework

Research shows that the brain develops five learning systems. Figure 1.1 portrays them graphically and illustrates how they are manifested in everyday life.

Emotional Learning System

In this book, you will be introduced to the *emotional learning system* first, because unless teachers establish a classroom climate conducive to emotional safety and personal relevancy for students, children will not learn effectively and may reject education altogether. Teachers who nourish the emotional system serve as *mentors* for students by demonstrating sincere enthusiasm for their subject; by helping students discover a passion for learning; by guiding them toward reasonable personal goals; and by supporting them in their efforts to become whatever they are capable of becoming. Without question, lessons need to be interesting, challenging, personally relevant, related to what students already know, and attainable within Vygotsky's (1978) "Zone of Proximal Development"—where students can independently complete tasks by learning the ability with the help of teachers, fellow students, or parents. When lessons satisfy these criteria, academic anxiety is minimized and the emotional system—and the student—is ready to learn.

Social Learning System

The natural propensities of the *social learning system* are the desires to belong to a group, to be respected, and to enjoy the attention of others. Whereas the emo-

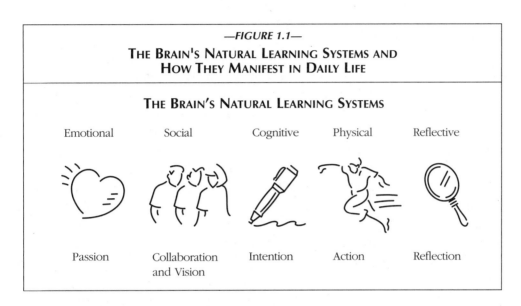

—*FIGURE 1.1*—
THE BRAIN'S NATURAL LEARNING SYSTEMS AND HOW THEY MANIFEST IN DAILY LIFE

THE BRAIN'S NATURAL LEARNING SYSTEMS

Emotional	Social	Cognitive	Physical	Reflective
Passion	Collaboration and Vision	Intention	Action	Reflection

tional system is personal, self-absorbed, and internal, the social system focuses on interaction with others or interpersonal experiences. Similarly, Rita Dunn and Kenneth Dunn (1992, 1993)—pioneers in learning styles research—identify the social system as one of five learning style domains. The Dunns' research focused on students' desire to work alone, with one other person, in small or large groups, and with congenial or authoritative adults as "elements of the social domain."

Students' social needs compel educators to organize schools into communities of learners where teachers and students can collaborate on authentic decision-making and problem-solving tasks. Within a community of learners, teachers and students relate to each other as a quasi-family structure where children receive respect and admiration for their strengths, whatever those strengths might be. By focusing on strengths in the classroom context, we recognize differences as individual gifts to be honored rather than as deficits to be corrected. This maximizes social growth through sincere collaboration of individuals whose differences contribute to creative problem-solving adventures. In such an atmosphere, the teacher collaborates with students as an equal partner in problem-solving adventures, rather than serve as a repository of information who stores and dispenses answers. The brain's social system either learns to promote authentic decision making by persons across ages, races, cultures, ethnicities, intellectual abilities, and academic skills, or it learns to view differences as liabilities. Herein lies one other critical role for teachers—to promote tolerance and understanding of diversity.

Cognitive Learning System

Throughout history, the brain's *cognitive learning system* has received the most attention because it pertains to reading, writing, calculation, and all other aspects of academic skill development. Even today, most standards for student learning—including the tests that measure them—focus on outputs of the cognitive learning system. Without attention to the other systems, however, students will be unable to achieve to their full potential.

Until the split-brain research made its imprint, teachers often taught discrete bits of information to be memorized rather than information patterns, concepts, and themes. When not making connections between new information and what students already know or the context in which it is found, teaching for memorization goes against how the cognitive learning system actually functions. This system flourishes when new information is embedded within thematic units of study that interrelate art, music, and physical activity within the real world of the student.

Attention to the cognitive system places teachers in the role of *learning facilitators* and students in the role of *authentic problem solvers and decision makers*. A facilitator sets the stage for learning. A facilitator does *not* tell or profess to know all the answers, but prepares the classroom with problems to be solved and arranges supporting materials for solutions as students address their need to know.

Physical Learning System

Learning also relies heavily on the *physical learning system*'s need to do things and students' propensity to be actively involved in learning. Though some students shy away from tactual (hands-on) and kinesthetic (movement and act-oriented) learning, others find learning enjoyable only when these modalities are engaged. The physical learning system likes challenging academic tasks that resemble a sport where teachers coach, inspire, and encourage active practice in the pursuit of success. The physical learning system needs to be actively engaged, because it cannot passively process information for later regurgitation on a test.

Reflective Learning System

Without the brain's *reflective learning system*, the work of the other four systems could produce limited results. This system involves personal consideration of one's own learning. It considers personal achievements and failures and asks what worked, what didn't, and what needs improvement. Knowledge of one's individual learning style and learning how to use style preferences can produce great academic gain (Dunn & Dunn, 1992, 1993). For example, if children know they learn best when new concepts are expressed as hands-on experiences, they can learn to translate information into manipulative resources, such as Task Cards, Electroboards, or Flip Chutes (Dunn & Dunn, 1992, 1993) (see Chapter 5 for further discussion of these resources). If children know they learn best by listening to stories about new information, then they can select books on a particular topic and request that they be recorded. The reflective learning system requires an understanding of one's self that can be developed through experimentation with different ways of learning. For example, keeping records of achievement and interpretation of ongoing progress give some indication of which learning systems or subsystems are most effective for an individual child. That is, children can learn to ask themselves, "Did I learn best when listening compared to reading, or handling information, or when working with others versus working alone?"

Although the reflective learning system is the last to develop biologically, it is the most human of all learning systems, acting as the brain's chief executive officer to integrate the organ's oldest and newest parts into a cohesive whole. Without explicit instruction in self-monitoring and performance analysis, however, this system can go dreadfully underdeveloped. Teachers, therefore, should act as *talent scouts* who identify student strengths. They then can guide and nurture student strengths to authentic gifts. This requires instructing students on how they learn and how to use their learning style preferences to develop strengths while transforming their weaknesses into challenging growth adventures.

Putting the Framework Together

The brain is a complex of widely and reciprocally interconnected systems. Systems theory allows us to study any part with the understanding that the brain is always interrelated with and dependent on larger and smaller systems. All five learning systems function simultaneously, and no system can be completely turned off, even though we may be conscious of only one system working at any one time.

Take the example of a chance meeting of friends at the grocery store. Brain chemicals called neurotransmitters rapidly signal neurons associated with each of the systems to fire or not to fire—say this and keep quiet about that. The cognitive system recalls the person's name, where they last saw one another, and how they first met. The emotional system reexperiences a measure of anxiety or pleasure depending on the conditions of their previous interactions. The social system provides standards of conduct: shake hands, hug, engage in nonthreatening conversation, ask about the kids. Inhibitory neurons of the physical system keep the friends standing in close proximity long enough for a chat before excitatory neurons stimulate movement for them to part. Later, when the friends share the chance meeting with others, the reflective system relives those moments mentally and ponders: "I wonder if I bragged about the kids too much" or "I wish it hadn't been a bad hair day."

The reflective analysis of the experience is a natural process that can become self-depreciating or self-aggrandizing. Neither is probably accurate to reality. Thus, the teacher's role is to teach youngsters how to look carefully at the evidence and reach conclusions based on facts, such as: "Without question, your multiplication skills are improving. Last week you completed four double-digit problems and today you worked six without difficulty." In school, therefore, record-keeping skills and analysis of those records need to be taught to properly develop the reflective learning system; otherwise, this system—and the student—may view the world in superficial ways and fail to fully develop.

Interaction between the various systems and subsystems signals the physical system to put down the milk before shaking hands and to move the lips so words can be spoken. Had any one of the systems been malfunctioning, the encounter would have taken on a totally different scenario: dropped groceries, stammering words, failure to recall the person's name, boisterous and inappropriate language, and so forth. Conceptually, no learning system stands alone. Each one's actions affect the others as part of a larger whole, like ripples from a handful of rocks tossed into a pond. As each rock forms its own ripples that bump and interfere with the others, the resulting combinations create a new overall wave pattern for the whole.

There is no question that distress from one of our learning systems can affect. For example, when upset with a loved one, concentration on paperwork seems impossible. When one is ill, it is difficult to feel romantic. When having a good time with friends, computing stock market returns is virtually impossible. Electrical currents, or wave action, from individual learning systems are thought to spread throughout the brain as one system interferes with or supports other learning systems. When teachers plan lessons and provide instruction, they must take each system into consideration, because each system of the brain is critical to the whole and cannot be ignored without detriment to the individual.

Other Approaches

Gardner's theory of multiple intelligences and various approaches to learning styles falls under the umbrella of learning systems. See Figure 1.2 for a comparison of three theoretical approaches to understanding human functioning. As noted, there is not a direct one-to-one match. For example, the reflective learning system considers all that is perceived within the environment, and it ponders thoughts and ideas. It also analyzes the past in relation to the present and anticipates and plans for the future. The reflective system is an overarching system, pondering the activity of all other systems. By contrast, Dunn and Dunn's environmental domain includes elements of individual preferences for bright or dim lighting, formal or informal furniture design, cool or warm climate, and quiet or sound when studying. The brain's reflective learning system is much more encompassing. When one considers comfort levels under various conditions, reflective learning is operating. Meanwhile, Gardner's "naturalist" intelligence suggests an affinity for understanding plants and wildlife and being at one with nature. According to the brain's natural learning systems concept, people who effectively converse with animals demonstrate high levels of social learning because they observe animal and plant behavior and respond positively to it. The naturalist intelligence suggests the ability to think about and reflect on nature. Thus, the theoretical overlap is present but not always evident.

Gardner and Veins (1990) maintain that a particular intelligence is used as needed, whereas a learning style is pervasive and influences how a person behaves across settings and circumstances. Silver, Strong, and Perini (2000) suggest that Gardner's multiple intelligences pertain to content (language, art, music) while learning styles focus on the process of learning. This reasonable distinction makes clear why the relationship between learning styles and learning systems is more robust than the relationship between multiple intelligences and the systems. According to the brain's natural learning systems framework, both the theory of multiple intelligences and the learning styles theory are small slices of a much larger pie. Multiple intelligences and various styles are embedded within the learning systems framework; learning systems are necessary for the construction of both, but neither is comprehensive enough to encompass the systems. Musical intelligence, for example, may require cognitive system attention when new material is being learned, but the emotional system takes over when a memorized piece is played with feeling and creativity. Similarly, conscious consideration is needed when learning to interact in

—*FIGURE 1.2*—

THREE THEORIES OF COGNITIVE FUNCTIONING: A COMPARISON AMONG BRAIN SYSTEMS, MULTIPLE INTELLIGENCES, AND LEARNING STYLES

The Brain's Natural Learning Systems	Gardner's Multiple Intelligences	Dunn & Dunn's Learning Style Domains
Emotional	Intrapersonal	Emotional
Social	Interpersonal	Social
Cognitive	Linguistic, Mathematical, Musical	Psychological
	Visual/Spatial	Physical
Physical	Bodily/Kinesthetic	
Reflective	Natural	Environmental

Source: Data from Gardner, H. (1983). Frames of Mind, New York, Basic Books and Dunn, R. & Dunn, K. (1993). Teaching Secondary Students through Their Individual Learning Styles. Boston: Allyn and Bacon.

accordance with the mores of a new culture, but as expected behaviors become automatic, the social system takes over so relationships can be established.

"Multiple intelligences" and "domains" are relatively new ways of viewing the complex nature of mental factors that impact learning. Before, J.P. Guilford (1967) had identified 120 different traits or modes of thought that he also categorized into operations, content, and products. Operations include cognition, memory, evaluation, convergent production, and divergent production; content factors include behavioral, visual figural, auditory figural, symbolic, and semantic; and product traits include what Guilford calls units, classes, relations, systems, transformations, and implications. Definitions of his terms are beyond the scope of this chapter, but it is interesting to note (as Perkins [1995] points out):

> Gardner. . . believes that the intelligences he proposes reflect in part underlying neurological factors. Second, several of Gardner's intelligences are not so different from those of Guilford's content dimension of intelligence. In particular, Guilford's figural (pictorial and spatial matters) matches

Gardner's spatial intelligence; his symbolic (numbers and notations) Gardner's logical-mathematical intelligence; and his semantic facet (words and ideas) Gardner's linguistic intelligence. (p. 75)

While Guilford bases his traits on statistical factor analysis, Gardner (1985) states that a "candidate intelligence" in his model "is reminiscent more of an artistic judgment than of a scientific assessment" (p. 63). Thus, any number of additional intelligences may be included in Gardner's model, as he noted: "There is not, and there can never be, a single irrefutable and universally accepted list of human intelligences. . . .We may come closer to this goal if we stick to only one level of analysis (say, neurophysiology) . . . ." (p. 60). This book advances such a neurophysiological approach. The five natural learning systems provide a framework or umbrella that supports a multitude of other "lists." Also, a total of five commonly understood systems is a manageable number to plan daily instruction. Within this framework, teachers can focus on specific "traits," "intelligences," or "domain elements" as the lesson objectives dictate.

Words of Caution

Research into the brain's natural learning systems holds high potential for curriculum development and lesson planning. However, John Bruer (1998, 1999) cautions educators not to leap to unsupported judgments regarding direct applications of neurobiological insights for educational applications. He chides educators who speak of "brain-based" learning as if using the brain for learning were a recent evolutionary wrinkle. He also criticizes educators who hold misconceptions of right-brain/left-brain behaviors and base educational practice on those misconceptions.

Clearly, some scientists make errors in timing, such as when prematurely disseminating preliminary split-brain results before all data are gathered and analyzed (Gazzaniga, 1985). Also, educators may attempt to fashion their lessons on a shallow understanding of what neuroscientists report. Despite these cautions, we still need to disseminate and pay attention to research even though we know that further investigation may suggest new directions. Dissemination informs further research and moves the field forward.

There is no question about the human brain's ability to learn. The problem for educators is the lack of a coherent framework based on brain research, which teachers can use to organize curricula and develop lesson plans linking what is taught with how the brain actually functions (Sylwester, 1995). Such a framework that supports the application of scientific insights to education can make the difference between students being identified as normally functioning or being labeled learning disabled, emotionally disturbed, or hyperactive. We now know enough about the brain to build that framework based on neuroscientific research that offers ample pegs of relevancy on which lesson planning and instruction can be hung. This book offers such a framework, built on the brain's natural learning systems to be a viable model of teaching and learning—a framework that bridges the gap between neuroscience and education.

2

The Emotional Learning System

More than any other system, the emotional learning system of the brain outwardly defines the individual and sets the stage for how people interact with others, learn, behave, and reflect on their circumstances. Scientists know that the most primitive need from birth, beyond physical nourishment for the body, is emotional nourishment for the soul. There is no doubt about it; *negative emotions* can definitely interfere with satisfactory academic achievement, whereas *positive emotions* can boost knowledge and skill acquisition. Nonetheless, negative emotions evolved "to activate our brain's attentional/problem solving systems so they (and not our emotions) can respond to a dangerous or opportunistic challenge. Our emotions are thus principally a sort of unconscious biological thermostat that recognize danger and trigger survival behaviors" (Sylwester, personal communication). For example, without acceptance and emotional support, energy needed for developing new skills may be spent seeking positive affirmations and guarding against abuse, ridicule, sarcasm, embarrassment, isolation, loneliness, and rejection.

Daniel Goleman (1995), author of *Emotional Intelligence*, states that emotionally upset people cannot remember, attend, learn, or make decisions clearly, because "stress makes people stupid" (p. 149). And Candace Pert (1993), author of *Molecules of Emotion*, points out that emotions link the body and brain and provide the energy that fuels academic achievement as well as personal health and success. "Everything we do," she said, "is run by emotions" (p. 187).

In support of Pert's views, Jaak Panksepp (1998), professor of psychobiology at Bowling Green State University, believes that our underlying emotional value systems are so powerful that, if they were destroyed, the cognitive apparatus could collapse. He notes that damage to emotional-limbic areas in young animals is much more devastating than damage to cognitive-neocortical areas. For example, an animal will show no sense of fear if the neural circuit between the amygdala and a particular area of the midbrain (the periaqueductal gray or PAG) is severed. That animal usually becomes another's dinner. An uncompromised circuit would alert the animal to danger and direct it to climb a tree, crouch low and remain still, or run for its life.

Structures of Emotion

Damage to specific areas of the human emotional system can be equally devastating as those in animals. For example, in *Descartes' Error*, Antonio Damasio (1994), head of the Department of Neurology at the University of Iowa College of Medicine, describes the change in a man's personality after an explosion forced a dynamite tamping rod through portions of his emotional structures. Before the accident, Phineas Gage was a mild-mannered, socially alert, clear-thinking railroad foreman, but became a foul-mouthed, argumentative, scattered thinker afterward. Damasio determined that the rod damaged some ventromedial portions of the most anterior aspects of the frontal cortex in the left and right hemispheres, and this damage is what changed Gage's behavior.

Conversely, frontal lobotomies can have a calming effect on people with high anxiety and volatile behavior (Carlson, 1995). However, after thousands of frontal lobe lobotomies were performed over the years, it finally became clear that severe personality changes that are less than desirable occurred. While intellectual performance remained unchanged, patients became "irresponsible and childish. They also lost the ability to carry out plans and most were unemployable. And although pathological emotional reactions were eliminated, so were normal ones" (p. 301). For example, after seeing a horrific accident, people with damaged frontal lobes can recall and describe details of the accident (e.g., "It was a disgusting image of a mutilated body"), but they display no emotional responses, only semantic ones (Gazzaniga, Ivry, & Mangun, 1998). Damasio (1994) concludes that connections between the ventromedial frontal cortex and the limbic system form a pathway that either mediates or helps to decipher physiological feelings.

Gazzaniga and colleagues (1998) determine that an understanding of the emotional process requires making distinctions at the molecular, cellular, and behavioral levels. They state:

At the molecular level, scientists use biochemical probes to identify sites where emotional information is processed. Once the site is identified, then cellular analysis is done to determine which neurons and synaptic connections mediate the emotion. Finally, at the behavioral level, populations of neurons and specialized circuits are linked to see how the whole brain participates in the behavior. (p. 514)

In part, emotions are chemical reactions to experiences that thwart or stimulate our desires—especially the desire to survive physically and psychologically. It is not yet clear where all the systems of emotion are located, but neurologist Joseph LeDoux (1996), author of *The Emotional Brain*, suggests that the major emotional systems of fear include the amygdala, the frontal cortex, and the cingulate cortex (semicircular structures that wrap around the mid portion of the brain known as the limbic area) (Figure 2.1). LeDoux identified visual and auditory neuronal pathways that go

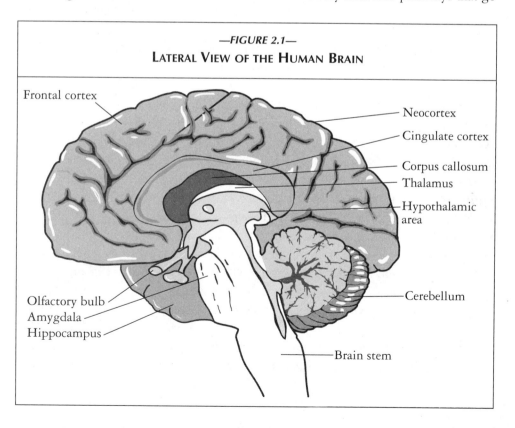

—*FIGURE 2.1*—
LATERAL VIEW OF THE HUMAN BRAIN

directly to the amygdala—almond-shaped structures found in each hemisphere toward the middle of the brain. The amygdala sends nerve fibers to the hypothalamus and brain stem, where breathing, sweating, heart rate, blood vessel, and muscle tone are controlled. The amygdala also receives input from the visual, auditory, and olfactory systems, as well as parts of the brain registering taste and touch.

Emotions also spread through various regions of the brain, which is where Panksepp (1998) thinks emotion is most likely distributed between higher levels of the brain, such as the frontal lobe, and lower areas, such as the brain stem. He suggests that these pathways serve executive functions for the emotional system. Although the major emotional systems and subsystems are arranged throughout much of the brain, most are located in the middle section—often called the limbic area—where they can coordinate the various emotional networks and circuits. Kawasaki (2001) and colleagues at the University of Iowa recently found that that neurons in the right prefrontal cortex distinguish or categorize emotional information received from visual input. Thus, the emotional learning system is a widespread, complex distributed neural system.

Some scientists continue to use Paul MacLean's (1990) conceptual model of the "triune brain" (three evolutionary layers) to locate emotional subsystems, even though others find it overly simplistic and outdated (LeDoux, 1996). On the basis of his theory that the brain develops in stages, MacLean identifies the oldest portion of the brain where fear, anger, and lust originated as the *reptilian brain*, because, according to evolution theory, it developed in reptiles and allowed them to protect their territories, fight or flee, find food, and procreate. MacLean termed the middle portion of the brain—located above the reptilian basal ganglia—the *mammalian brain*, because it is where the social emotions related to maternal acceptance, care, social bonding, separation distress, and rough-and-tumble play are programmed. MacLean refers to the thinking portion of the brain, which molds expression of the other two parts, as the *neocortex* or new brain because it evolved last (Panksepp, 1998). More recently, Eshter Sternberg (2000), director of the Molecular, Cellular, and Behavioral Integrative Neuroscience Program and chief of the Neuroendocrine Immunology and Behavior Section at the National Institute of Mental Health of the National Institutes of Health, praises LeDoux's identification of vision-to-fear and hearing-to-fear pathways, which are processed through the amygdala. She believes similar pathways exist for the pleasure center, called the nucleus accumbens and located deep within the brain. "There are parts of the brain," Sternberg says, "that control those positive emotional and physiological components of the thing we call love: pleasure, happiness, warmth, and comfort, as well as the set of sexual responses we associate with romantic love" (p. 35). We know less about the nucleus accumbens than the amygdala, but both are linked by nerve pathways to the frontal lobe and the hippocampus, which coordinate centers of thought and memory (Sternberg). Therefore, emotions cannot be ignored as critical to the learning process.

Functions of Emotion

The brain—and thus, the emotional system—operates electrophysiologically, neurochemically, and behaviorally (Panksepp, 1998). The *electrophysical* system generates its own electrical voltage to transport information from neuron to neuron by converting brain chemistry into nerve impulses or *action potentials* that travel down the long neuronal axons. When the electrical impulse reaches the axon terminal, calcium enters through small pores in the cell's membrane. Together, the calcium and nerve impulse force chemicals (neurotransmitters) from tiny cargo vesicles to fire. The neurotransmitters then electrochemically slingshot from the axon terminals to the tiny spaces between neurons called *synapses*, which the neurotransmitters swim across and temporarily lodge in receptors located on dendrites of receiving neurons. Once their chemical message-in-a-bottle is delivered, the neurotransmitters move back into synapse. At that point, one of three things might happen:

1. Enzymes deactivate the neurotransmitter.
2. The neurotransmitter returns to the sending neuron to reabsorb calcium.
3. Chemicals called *peptides* slowly modulate and degrade the synaptic activity.

Depending on where they are located within the brain, neurons may fire from a few times per second to hundreds of times per second, just as some people talk a lot or a little. Slower-paced neurons are abundant in the emotional, hypothalamic-limbic regions of the brain, while some neurons do not fire at all unless the right environmental stimulus comes along (Panksepp, 1998). Neurons for rage, as noted earlier, may never have reason to exercise their power.

The behavioral aspects of emotion can be stimulated by external input such as sight, sound, smell, or other sensory experiences, or by thoughts such as, "I feel all alone; nobody likes me" and "What a great day! Life is truly beautiful!" A coordinated brain/body state fluctuates markedly as a function of time and with changes in events and the appraisal of events (Panksepp, 1998). Whether stimulated internally or externally, the activated circuits use learning and past emotions as a gradient against which to filter all input and generate physiological changes *simultaneously throughout the brain and body* (Dozier, 1998). These changes dictate what is worthy of attention, concerted energies, and motivated engagement within all bombarding information.

Scientists categorize emotions differently. For example, Damasio (1999) distinguishes between *primary, secondary,* and *background* emotions. *Primary* or universal emotions include happiness, sadness, fear, anger, surprise, and disgust; they are found in all cultures around the world. *Secondary* or social emotions include embarrassment, jealousy, guilt, and pride and depend on cultural interpretations. *Background* emotions, by contrast, include well-being or malaise and calm or tension, and they tend to partially correspond to an individual's temperament (see Figure 2.2).

Panksepp (1998) categorizes emotions based on their time of emergence. For example, he states that the mammalian brain has four innate (genetic) emotional systems that mature soon after birth—seeking, fear, rage, and panic—and three more that emerge later—love, grief, and play. Because seeking, fear, and rage frequently create difficulties for schoolchildren, they are the focus of this chapter.

Seeking

Affective neural systems contribute to feelings of engagement and excitement as humans seek material resources for survival and when we pursue interests that bring positive meaning into our lives (Panksepp, 1998). The neurotransmitter dopamine is especially important for energizing a person into seeking activity. Without it, Panksepp believes "human aspirations remain frozen in an endless winter of discontent" (p. 144); thought and action seem to remain at a standstill. Dopamine is associated with the feeling tone of invigorated anticipation of thrills and other rewards so powerful that animals and humans will work to artificially activate this emotional system electrically or chemically (Panksepp). For example, rats wired to trigger dopamine production in their brains will self-stimulate by repeatedly pushing a lever until they drop from exhaustion. Similarly, we have heard of addicts who steal from their mothers, abuse and neglect their children, and sell their possessions to obtain the stimulation of cocaine and amphetamines. In fact, the

---

—FIGURE 2.2—

ADVERSITY OFTEN REVEALS DEEP-SEATED TEMPERAMENT AND CHARACTER TRAITS

Temperament and Character

J.F. leaned forward in her wheelchair to manipulate the long-handled paintbrush clutched confidently between her teeth. With focused attention she guided each stroke's appearance upon the canvas until her wondrous work was finally complete. She sat back, admired the pale grays, blues, and muted pinks that carefully accentuated the pen and ink drawing of a young migrant worker and her baby. Later, as J.F. rode to work in the back of her specially built van, she joked with her driver/attendant about his driving and said she might have to get behind the wheel and wouldn't that be a hoot.

As a University of Virginia freshman on that fateful day 6 years earlier, J.F. stood up from sunbathing on the third-floor balcony and fell to the ground as the railing gave way. I went to the hospital a few days after the accident, and there she lay without the voluntary use of any part of her body except her face and mouth muscles, some neck movement, slight activity in her right shoulder, and a few finger movements. Yet, a smile crossed her lips and she greeted me as if we were old friends. She and her mother quietly bantered with one another as she sipped her water and asked that a contrary strand of hair be pushed from her eye.

I met J.F. only once before when she came to the university to see her mother, a treasured colleague whose quick wit, positive affect, and laughter kept everyone in a good mood. In that one meeting, J.F.'s beautiful personality and authentic charm were stunning. Those same qualities radiated from her hospital bed, whereas tears flowed from my eyes as I sat in puzzled silence unable to start the car's engine and return home.

Clearly, my ability to handle adversity—even when it was not my own—crumbled and paled in comparison to what I had just witnessed. I wondered then and continue to ask, what in J.F.'s emotional learning system of temperament, personality, and character allowed her mood to be so positive even at her darkest hour? How could her mother remain so confident that everything would work out as her hopes, dreams, and desires for her daughter lay motionless on that hospital bed?

---

addictive effects of cocaine and other agents of abuse are caused by increased levels of dopamine in critical brain regions involved in motivation and emotional reinforcement (Purves et al., 2001).

Even though the dopamine-seeking action potential is built into our brains, it varies from person to person. Each animal or person, however, learns to direct behavior toward available opportunities in the environment that cause the brain to produce dopamine (Panksepp, 1998). In moderate amounts, the chemical *drives* and *energizes* motivation and persistence, stimulating curiosity, the need for interesting experiences, sensation seeking, and efforts to grasp higher meanings of life. In other words, it helps connect the world of experience with the world of ideas in cause-and-effect fashion. In moderately high amounts, dopamine produces a sense of excitement, creative imagination, and inspiration; however, overproduction can produce schizophrenia or manic behavior. Some people elect to stimulate high levels of dopamine by choosing adventurous activities—they are referred to as *novelty seekers*—while others shy away from behavior that creates the physiological and emotional responses generated by dopamine.

Novelty seekers get excited about ideas and new sensations, such as watching leaves cascading from towering oaks, examining stimulating artwork, walking the high wire, and engaging in exotic travel or counterculture experiences. They like to meet new people. By contrast, those low on this trait enjoy old acquaintances, even if they do not like them much (Hamer & Copeland, 1998). Whereas novelty seekers are curious, impulsive, extravagant, disorderly, and enthusiastic, people low on this trait tend to be indifferent, reflective, frugal, orderly, and regimented (Hamer & Copeland). Students with a high novelty-seeking trait are high risk takers who deplore repetition, routine, and boring people; those low on this trait prefer order and discipline and want things to remain the same. *The challenge is to prepare an educational environment that provides routine while introducing some measure of academic risk taking.*

Studies from Dean Hamer's biochemistry lab at the National Cancer Institute demonstrate that in terms of novelty seeking, people prefer working with others like themselves (Hamer & Copeland, 1998). That is, those high in novelty seeking want to work with others who are high on this trait while low novelty seekers prefer working with others who are low on this trait. The desire to work with others like themselves is also demonstrated by Milgram, Dunn, and Price (1993), who found that adolescents prefer working with others like themselves in terms of interests and learning style.

These findings raise questions about how teachers should organize children for small group activities. For example, many cooperative learning advocates recommend that groups include students who represent a mixture of cognitive abilities, gender, and academic skills without consideration of their novelty-seeking levels or learning style preferences. Teachers should reconsider his recommendation, however, when assigning work to the group. Perhaps allowing like-minded students to work together would be more fruitful in certain cases. Once students learn the conduct of collaboration and cooperative skills, teachers could introduce a broader diversity of ideas.

Fear and Anxiety

Whereas "seeking" behavior is associated with a specific neurotransmitter, fear and anxiety are much more complex in both their operational structures and the various neurotransmitters involved. Fear—a primary emotion for human survival—evolves in the limbic or mammalian area of the brain and connects with the six-layered cerebral cortex for interpretation of incoming sensory information (Panksepp, 1998; Pinker, 1997). This partnership between the emotional and cognitive systems rapidly produces an emotional first impression of everything we experience; that input is monitored with regard to whether we like or dislike it. When the dislike is intense, the primitive fear reaction of flight or fight is triggered (Dozier, 1998).

Sometimes we are aware of the interpretation process going on, but at other times we are not. Within thousandths of a second, a major form of trepidation focuses the sensory input and links it with memory systems that consciously or unconsciously ask, "Am I in danger? Do I need to run or fight?" Various neurotransmitters are triggered, and, dependent upon the intensity of concern, feelings from anxiety to fear result (Panksepp, 1998).

Anxiety is fear of the future. With traumatic national events and society's fast-paced environment, teachers and their students "can feel sudden onsets of anxiety or even panic and chalk them up to personality characteristics like being 'hyper' or 'edgy' when they may be automatic fear reactions to environmental elements" (Dozier, 1998, p. 147). Unless the fears are overt, feelings of anxiety may never be associated with some level of fear.

As if anxiety weren't enough to shut down learning, children often watch scary movies or television programs that continue to frighten them for weeks or months. I still recall how the ugly witch in *Snow White* haunted my thoughts for years and caused me to look with suspicion on any woman dressed entirely in black. Yet, adolescents and adults often deliberately trigger fear reactions by attending horror movies, watching violent TV programs, and reading "thrillers" that vicariously produce survival reactions. As Dozier (1998) so forcefully pointed out even before the televised repetitions of the World Trade Center attack, the steady stream of crime scenes and reports of violence on the news and in television programming can dampen the primitive fear system while simultaneously increasing one's anxieties about what might happen to us or our loved ones under similar circumstances.

On a less dramatic but equally anxiety-producing level, students who cannot follow the rate of their teacher's speech or keep up with the discussion may become anxious in class for fear the teacher will call on them. They may suffer anxiety caused by fear of being bullied by bigger students, or by the fear of being socially isolated by classmates who push them into behavior they regret. Even being accepted into a group can create its own anxieties—produced by fear of future loss of that affiliation (Dozier, 1998).

A steady diet of fear, either triggered through actual events or generated vicariously, dramatically diminishes a person's ability to use other learning systems effectively. The body and brain must busily cope with unrelenting stress chemicals that limit their ability to produce and process more healthy chemicals. Further, the outward manifestations of personal fear can be masked as misbehavior, nonresponsiveness, lack of motivation, and other chronic behavior patterns. These traits may look like a negative attitude, rather than a coping strategy against the fear of failure, the fear of social isolation, the fear of an angry parent, or any number of other fears that children fail to understand and cannot effectively articulate.

Fear *is* an authentic emotion, and how teachers respond to students' fears is important not just for the present, but also for the lifetime of the child. If unchecked, fear can lead to phobias, irrational anxieties, panic attacks, obsessive-compulsive disorder, paranoia, and post-traumatic stress syndrome (Dozier, 1998). In fact, chronic negative feelings, limited academic engagement, and frequent disruptive behavior may have their roots in childhood traumas. Similarly, chronic disruptive behavior may be symptoms of chronic stress syndrome resulting from ongoing responses to more subtle fears.

The emotion of fear is exceedingly powerful in children's lives, even with mild forms of fear such as anxiety and high levels of harm avoidance. Because youngsters are hesitant to admit to being anxious or afraid, educators need to create safe schooling environments where taunting, teasing, and isolation are unacceptable.

Harm avoidance. Generally viewed as a "temperament trait" generating fear, anxiety, worry, neuroticism, and emotional sensitivity, harm avoidance is caused by a "prickly anxiety and a deeply negative worldview that colors everything . . . . It is a fear of life itself . . . . life is dark, the future is grim, and every day is a drag"

(Hamer and Copeland, 1998, p. 55). Students low in harm avoidance demonstrate an uninhibited, carefree, calm, and secure outlook on life, and are often viewed as student leaders. Meanwhile, those high in harm avoidance may be fearful of new classroom experiences and move away from attempting new things.

Jerome Kagan (1994) of Harvard University believes inherited differences in the amygdala—the brain's storage center for emotional memories—play a key role in harm avoidance. Kagan found that electroencephalograms (EEGs) of hundreds of children demonstrated greater activity in the right frontal lobe of those with high levels of harm avoidance, while their cheerful, bold counterparts showed more left-side activity. This is important—the right hemisphere is associated with controlling negative emotions, whereas the left is associated with positive emotions.

Harm avoidance is one of the earliest expressed, most persistent, and most enduring aspects of temperament, normally showing up as shyness and inhibition (Hamer & Copeland, 1998). Further, chemical analysis of saliva from shy girls revealed two times more cortisol—a brain-produced stress hormone—than did the saliva of bold girls (Hamer & Copeland). Some evidence, however, suggests that this trait can be changed. Goleman (1995) reports that when parents of shy children deliberately encourage gregarious behavior in respectful ways, children largely overcome their trepidations. Through kind humor and good-natured classroom interactions that honor children and opportunities to see "failures" as feedback for progress and growth, teachers can go a long way toward helping children replace their patterns of fear and anxiety with confidence and eager anticipation.

Another method of lowering anxiety and harm avoidance is to fulfill proper dietary needs. Limited intake of protein can cause students to appear shy and withdrawn due to a lack of phenylalanine and tyrosine needed to trigger dopamine, norepinephrine, and epinephrine (Wurtman, 1988). Students—and teachers—who come to school with inadequate protein in their diets tend to be sleepy, sullen, and lacking in motivation and may behave in shy, harm-avoiding ways (Howard, 1994; Wurtman). By contrast, Hamer and Copeland (1998) report that people demonstrating high levels of harm avoidance are low in the neurotransmitter serotonin, whereas those high in serotonin were low on the harm avoidance trait.

One way to increase the production of serotonin is by providing crackers, bagels, toast, pretzels, raw vegetables, and other complex carbohydrates to children throughout the school day (Wurtman & Suffes, 1996/1997). Conversely, students who are sluggish and sleepy may require more protein intake. Modification of diet, therefore, may be an important intervention. Unfortunately, school lunches often consist of snacks high in sugar content and limited nutritional value. Further, teachers who reward children with candy should expect brief periods of alert behaviors quickly followed by sluggishness. Dispensing candy at school should be against educational policy.

Anger and Rage

Rage is an intense form of anger, and anger is "that powerful brain force we experience as an internal pressure to reach out and strike someone" (Panksepp, 1998, p. 187). Rage occurs as a result of being stuck in a *fear-flight* response when attempts to flee a fearful situation are thwarted. Although relatively few people actually have been caught in a burning building or a sinking ship, we can easily imagine the strong forces driving our survival behavior. For instance, if a parent holds a baby's arms at her sides so she cannot move, the baby will quickly sense frustration, soon followed by anger and an aggressive struggle. Failure to free the baby's arms will escalate her reaction to frantic wailing and thrashing about in full-blown rage.

This trapped sensation can be psychological as well as physical, such as when feeling betrayed. The psychological sense of being unable to flee can also produce bodily reactions associated with rage: the face flushes; breathing is shallow and rapid; there may be agitated pacing that resembles a stomping walk rather than a thoughtful stroll; the urge to hit is nearly uncontrollable; and the feeling of being a caged animal is overwhelming. When "cornered" physically or psychologically, a generally peaceful person can strike out with strong verbal assaults, kicking, clawing, scratching, and biting.

The actual brain mechanisms that control anger are complex and only roughly understood, because multiple physiological, neuroanatomical, and neurochemical factors control them (Panksepp, 1998). Further, neuroscientists cannot yet identify the relationship of cultural, environmental, and cognitive causes of anger and aggression. Media reports of an "aggression gene" may be overblown, even though genetic sociopathic tendencies exist (Hamer & Copeland, 1998). For example, families with a history of serious aggression seem to have an abundance of a specific enzyme that breaks down serotonin and other biogenic amines. Humans with high levels of this enzyme have constitutionally low levels of serotonin activity. These people act out frustration far more than those with higher levels of serotonin

(Linnoila et al., 1994). High levels of norepinephrine also increase the general arousal effects of anger and aggression.

Conversely, dietary deprivation of complex carbohydrates can produce an inadequate supply of tryptophan and a limited quantity of the neurotransmitter serotonin. These short supplies can result in hyperexcitability, a sense of anxiety, and edginess (Panksepp, 1998). One reason ice cream is such a favorite food is that the simple sugars trigger an almost instant surge of serotonin, which calms anxieties and produces feelings of relaxation, at least momentarily (Wurtman & Suffes, 1996/1997). Diet can act as a booster or trigger for chemical production of intact systems.

In addition, low serotonin activity is highly correlated with delinquency in human males, whereas socially successful male leaders have high brain serotonin activity (Panksepp, 1998). Panksepp reports that serotonin supplements reduce aggression and irritability when given to animals whose serotonin activity is decreased because of social isolation. Serotonin is a critical hormone neurotransmitter in terms of aggression, and, as noted earlier, it can be increased by diet, which is discussed in Chapter 5.

Strengthening Emotional Pathways. Just as exercise makes our muscles stronger and disuse makes them weaker, experiences change the quantitative expressions of neural systems (Panksepp, 1998). Expressions of anger, therefore, may increase the brain's circuits for anger. Acting out our anger may be the worst thing we can do, because venting can escalate into rage (Hamer & Copeland, 1998). Acting out a frustration can lead from anger to hostility, impulsive retaliation, full-fledged crime, or other antisocial behavior when least expected. Perhaps this helps explain the desire to kick the vending machine when it takes our money without producing a desired snack, or the upsurge of "road rage" by normally peaceful people.

Without specific training to the contrary, children quickly learn to appraise the sources of their frustrations. By exercising their human propensity to blame, they then "fault" others for making them angry. Negative attitudes directed toward one person are often projected onto anyone who generates feelings of frustration, disgust, or anger. If this blame cycle is repeatedly played out and reinforced with positive or negative consequences, children reduce their willingness to assume personal responsibility. As a consequence, their refusal may become a "hard-wired" behavior pattern.

Just because anger is natural, we are not compelled to give in to it. If teachers have difficulty controlling their own frustration and anger, teaching anger control to their students is virtually impossible. Emotional and cognitive habits that control anger and harness it productively can be developed (Hamer & Copeland, 1998). The neural rage circuit actually allows for a wide range of behavioral control, because it, as well as other emotional circuits, is open to higher-order executive functions of the neocortex. Habits can be developed and employed to control the nature of pre-existing functions. That is, as we mature, we can choose to be angry or not; we learn to "pick our battles" wisely.

The progression from frustration, anger, impulsiveness, aggression, hostility, and rage to actual violence is one of the most critical issues we face as a society, and it is one that educators must deal with in students—and sometimes them-selves—on a daily basis (Hamer & Copeland, 1998). We need to teach anger man-agement as a lifelong strategy that can benefit society. Learning to control one's emotions is even more important than academic skill development for students whose behavior is out of control. Of course, part of their anger may result from a lack of skill development commensurate with their classmates and friends, so aca-demics cannot be ignored either. Consequently, the curriculum must include strate-gies for personal growth in both the academic and emotional areas.

Personality

"Of all the things we learn and remember in life, the most important is who we are" (Hamer & Copeland, 1998). The concept of self—how we think about our-selves—is a combination of genetic predispositions and how we mold those pre-dispositions into rather consistent behavior and thought patterns. Our somewhat stable reactions to the primal emotions of seeking, fear, anger, and other primary emotions manifest as characteristics, such as being shy or bold, cheerful or somber, impulsive or reflective, introverted or extroverted, fearful or calm, and other tem-peramental traits (Hamer & Copeland).

The portion of personality that is genetically hardwired goes with us from one setting to the next, but feelings and the behavior generated from them are contex-tually specific. For instance, if we are shy or bold in one setting, we tend to be shy or bold across settings. By contrast, in school a child's sense of self may be one of worthlessness, whereas outside the school setting the same child may feel honored by family members and of great value to the community. Damasio (1999) makes a clear distinction between emotion and feeling with the following statement:

It is through feelings, which are inwardly directed and private, that emotions, which are outwardly directed and public, begin their impact on the mind; but the full and lasting impact of feelings requires consciousness, because only along with the advent of a sense of self do feelings become known to the individual having them . . . . I separate three stages of processing along a continuum: *a state of emotion*, which can be triggered and executed nonconsciously; *a state of feeling*, which can be triggered and executed nonconsciously; and *a state of feeling made conscious*, i.e., known to the organism having both emotion and feeling. (pp. 36–37)

A *concept of self* includes the level to which a person takes responsibility for his or her actions in response to emotions and feelings. Damasio (1999) stresses that responsibility for one's actions requires consciousness, even though primitive emotions evolved long before it, as we will discuss in Chapter 4. The link between emotions and consciousness, therefore, underscores a point made later: Learning systems function in parallel and depend on one another for expression. This is certainly true in terms of one's concept of self.

If a person attributes personal behavior, success, and failure to hard work, determination, decision making, and persistence, there is a high level of personal responsibility. If the person attributes behavior, success, and failure to forces outside his control, such as "the teacher's fault," bad luck, or what others did or did not do, then he avoids responsibility and limits persistence. If educators expect students to persevere with learning tasks, then they must attend to how students view themselves within the classroom context.

The concept of self develops as individuals interpret their own thoughts and actions in relation to their inner drives. They then define themselves based on those mental and physical behaviors. For example, if students frequently act out and are abrasive or belligerent, their own actions become internalized as defining characteristics of self as "difficult." By contrast, if students see themselves as friendly, helpful, and kind, those characteristics become internalized as a definition of self as "pleasant and caring." Students then continue to behave in ways consistent with their self-perception.

The reactions of others, particularly parents and teachers in a child's young years and peers during teenage years, provide psychological mirrors for helping children interpret their own identity. The teacher's role is to systematically work toward instilling positive behavior by using subtle techniques without pressure or insistence. For example, a young child may begin to view himself as a "thief" and then live up to that concept of self if he is punished too harshly for taking something that belongs to someone else. By contrast, if an understanding adult or peer treats the "theft" as an opportunity for the child to develop delayed gratification, honesty, truthfulness, and character, then the same child could learn from his mistakes and develop more socially appropriate behavior. In fact, transgressions may serve as a springboard for personal goal setting that capitalizes on the child's strengths and emotional passions.

Goal Setting

Goal setting is a conscious act of the cognitive learning system, but to be effective, it should be based on a student's passion for learning or accomplishing something specifically meaningful to him or her. When students' academic and personal goals become an integral part of the curriculum, they know that what they feel passionate about is valued; students will sense that they are important to others simply because they are who they are. Their psychological need to be themselves, therefore, encourages them to explore their strengths rather than focus on their weaknesses. Also, when students openly discuss their goals and teachers integrate them in the curriculum, this public airing increases a sense of ownership of what is being taught and makes the likelihood of goal fruition much more probable (Cialdini, 1984).

Everyone's primary goals are all about the same: to survive physically and psychologically; and to be comfortable, accepted, loved, and respected. If issues at home or school block these goals, it is tough for students to concentrate on math and spelling lessons. The long-term goal of becoming a proficient speller, for example, is temporarily forgotten when a student feels emotional distress. At that point, impulse control and self-regulation give way to immediate self-indulgent behavior. "People seek to feel better immediately, and to accomplish that, they yield to temptations even when doing so may be contrary to their long-term best interests and self-regulatory goals," Dianne Tice and her colleagues (2001) write in the *Journal of Personality and Social Psychology*.

When primary goals of "seeking" are reasonably satisfied, we can focus on realizing our personal potential, or what psychologist Abraham Maslow calls self-actualization. Mihaly Csikszentmihalyi (1993), author of *The Evolving Self: A Psychology for the Third Millennium*, adds, "The value of the goal is simply that it offers an opportunity to use and refine one's abilities. It does not have to have any monetary or social value. . . .When we enjoy it, it is because we think of it as something that allows us to express our potential, to learn about our limits, to stretch our being ... it is a self-communication" (p. 180).

Nature versus Nurture

Although there is no clear way of knowing what the percentage of nature and nurture mix is, Debra Niehoff (1999), a Johns Hopkins-educated neuroscientist and biomedical communications professional, reports a 40- to 60-percent variation in temperament and personality traits that can be attributed to genetic factors. She maintains that nature is revealed in personality and learning style beginning at birth "in the form of individual variation in responsiveness, intensity, ability to adapt to change, reactions to novelty—traits that collectively define the characteristic approach to the world known as temperament and that are demonstrably sensitive to genetic influence" (p. 45).

By contrast, in his book *The Feeling of What Happens*, Antonio Damasio (1999) states that it is foolhardy to argue the role of nature versus nurture in the creation of the emotional self. "Notwithstanding the reality that learning and culture alter the expression of emotions and give emotions new meanings," he stresses, "emotions are biologically determined processes, depending on innately set brain devices, laid down by a long evolutionary history" (p. 51). How environment shapes these genetically determined processes varies across individuals and circumstances.

Although the mix of genetics and environmental influences is unclear, the environment unquestionably influences expression of the range in genetic predispositions. For example, the genetic predisposition for rage may never be triggered because of lack of exposure to triggering circumstances or because of environmental training. The effect of schooling on emotion and learning, therefore, cannot be overstated. Emotion prompts thought, and many thoughts evoke emotions (Panksepp, 1998). Conflict resolution and peer mediation curricula are important in this regard; they teach children to think of alternate, positive reactions to situations that might prompt rage or other negative emotions.

Educational Considerations

In this chapter, I have discussed three primal emotions: seeking, fear, and anger. Each emotion motivates students in negative and positive ways, and educators need to be aware that these motivations can affect their students' personalities, and in turn, their learning ability.

Seeking is a natural emotion that motivates behavior. In the classroom, students' individual desires, dreams, and expectations lead to personal goal setting. Because children often have difficulty articulating ideas and activities they feel passionate about, teachers need to include lesson plans for developing personal goals. Both teachers and students then can develop workable plans for reaching these goals. Further, all aspects of the curriculum can be linked to individual goals, thus giving them purpose and meaning. Fear and anxiety can motivate students toward harm avoidance or risk taking, just as the neuronal rage circuit can motivate children to take responsibility for their own actions or blame someone else when things fail to work out as they desire. In fact, aggression and fear overlap in many areas of the brain even though they have distinct emotional systems. When people are fearful, aggression tends to rise. With comfort, aggression decreases. This tendency may help explain why there is much less aggression in relationships among people who know one another well versus those who are strangers (Panksepp, 1998). The lesson here is that classrooms and whole schools need to be places where teachers and students know and care for one another, respecting each other's personal strengths and helping to diminish their weaknesses.

Learning depends on *emotional state*, which determines to what we pay attention and what we learn. Consequently, teachers cannot ignore emotion as a vital influence in the learning process. Teachers who understand the links between emotions and learning can help students use their emotions productively in assessing situations and taking actions that clarify individual strengths, set personally relevant goals, resolve conflicts, manage anger, and express emotions in socially acceptable ways. Without question, emotions are linked to attitude, motivation, persistence, perseverance, and self-worth. Thus, emotion drives personal qualities that dramatically affect a student's success or failure at school.

Teachers must be careful to read the body language and emotional states of their students and interact with them accordingly. For example, when a student feels sad, the teacher needs to match the tone of sadness. If the teacher were to ignore the emotional state of sadness and introduce a lesson with gung-ho enthusiasm, chances are great that child would react with disinterest or even anger. Similarly, whole classes may exhibit a pervasive tone of disinterest and lethargy, such as an "I'd rather be any place in the world but here" attitude. Teachers who attempt to combat lethargy with flaming enthusiasm may find students sinking further down into their seats.

By contrast, teachers who begin their lessons slowly in a low-key manner and gradually increase their own enthusiasm have a greater chance of bringing the class along the same well-measured crescendo. Teachers must metaphorically walk in step with the emotions of students. Once this process—called entrainment—is achieved, teachers can move students slowly to different social-emotional states. But while matching states is important, it is not always easy to accomplish. A keen sense of *compassionate* humor is an invaluable asset for teachers to cultivate because it can ease tension that may exist because of a mismatch between the teacher's and students' emotional states. There is no room in compassionate humor, however, for subtle or overt sarcasm that some teachers employ in a difficult situation. Such action is clearly bound to backfire at the moment or over time because sarcasm is a humorous put-down at someone else's expense.

Although emotions can overpower cognition, they can also enhance learning. "We remember only those things we feel something about whether the feeling is fear, hunger, or desire" (Dozier, 1998, p. 43). Both Goleman (1995) and Damasio (1994, 1999) argue that when choices need to be made, the emotional learning system sends signals to the cognitive learning system. These signals streamline decision making by eliminating some options and highlighting others at the outset. In this way, the emotional brain is just as involved in reasoning as is the thinking brain, and educators must teach accordingly.

Keeping the Emotional Learning System in Balance

As emphasized earlier, the brain's emotional learning system strives for personal relevance and opportunities to become a unique individual with hopes, dreams, and aspirations that may or may not appeal to anyone else. When the psychological "need to be me" is met, this system generates *passion* for becoming all you are capable of becoming.

Students of equal initial abilities can become excellent—or hopeless—in a subject depending on their love or hatred of it. Passion is incorporated into the biological tissues of the brain just as are consistent patterns of thought, sense of self, and negative or positive feelings. Because passion breeds talent, teachers possess considerable power to help children develop positive attitudes toward learning (Dehaene, 1997). Emotions, not cognitive stimulation, serve as the mind's primary architect for constructing its highest capacities: intelligence, morality, and sense of self (Greenspan, 1997). Thus, teachers who support and nurture students' individual needs serve as *mentors* and *models*, motivating and encouraging expression of their students' internally generated passion.

Conversely, a person functioning predominantly in the emotional learning system produces an egocentric worldview. This self-absorption becomes prevalent during adolescence; unless teachers and other adults take measures to move students to a less egocentric perspective, it may linger into adulthood. Because of this possibility, we must engage middle and high school students in service-learning projects. For example, when older students listen to emerging readers practice their skills, when they assume maintenance tasks to keep the school clean, or when they read their compositions to the elderly, they are learning to look beyond themselves while feeling a sense of personal importance.

If students shut down their emotional learning systems, they find little joy in learning, little satisfaction in developing new skills, and no fun from activities other students approach with glee. Sullen, passive, withdrawn, and defiant students may suffer from extreme emotional pain that forces them to repress their feelings or to strike out at others in passive or aggressive ways. These youngsters require a positive reawakening of their emotional systems in a psychologically safe environment where all are respected and honored. They require opportunities to be successful and to know they are special just for being themselves. A service project that involves the care of injured or abused animals can go a long way toward helping physically and mentally abused children regain a sense of emotional strength.

A curriculum rich in personal relevance is essential for nurturing the emotional learning system and helping heal students' emotional wounds. For example, when students study about specific individuals involved in a historic event, class speculations about how that person felt—what fears, sadness, or longings could have propelled him or her to action—provide emotional perspectives to which students can relate without feeling personally singled out. Further, teachers can use "The Ugly Duckling" and other fairy tales that are rich in metaphor to help young children identify with the characters. The tales can also promote analytical skills in adolescents and smooth the transition from childhood to emerging maturity (Mills & Crowley, 1986). Students can legitimately relive their past while making personal connections with the characters in more mature ways. Emotions then can be discussed at a distance through the story characters rather than in a straightforward fashion, which is generally awkward for students.

◆　　◆　　◆

The brain's emotional learning system is demanding. It must feel comfortable before the mind can engage in cognitive learning. Self-absorption, however, cannot be allowed to take over the individual. The emotional learning system must attain a balance between emotional shutdown and self-absorption. It also must attain balance with the other four systems to achieve a comprehensive sense of personal comfort and well-being.

When emotions are positive, teachers and students feel good about school. They take responsibility for teaching and learning, they persevere until tasks are complete, and they accept standards of learning as a viable challenge and tackle them with vigor. In so doing, they create a harmonious social learning milieu where deep learning can take place, and they feel free to express themselves honestly in terms of their own personalities. Clearly, individuals and society benefit when teachers use their emotions effectively to increase achievement and promote the quality of their lives and the lives of students. Perhaps emotional nourishment for the soul is what schooling is really about.

3

The Social Learning System

The study of social learning is emerging as a critical area of neurobiological investigation. In fact, researchers have identified several neural structures and chemistries that relate to specific social needs and social emotions; however, much of what we might say about the social subsystems is speculative.

Structures of Social Learning

Research suggests that the right hemisphere is more important than the left for social interactions. Although social skills are not localized in any one part of the cerebral cortex, much has been learned about the importance of the orbitofrontal cortex for social judgments, as seen in the case of Phineas Gage's accident.

The orbitofrontal cortex covers the brain just above the bones that form the eye sockets or *orbits*, hence the term *orbitofrontal* (Carlson, 1995). Fontal lobe lobotomies take place in this area. When lesions occur in this part of the brain, aggressive animals become so docile they no longer showed fear of their natural enemies. For instance, Carlson reports on the work researchers did with a chimpanzee named Becky in 1935. She had violent temper tantrums whenever she responded to tests incorrectly; she rolled on the floor, defecated and urinated, and failed to respond to additional tasks. After removal of the frontal lobe, Becky became a model student, but failed to register any emotion to her natural enemies such as snakes. After undergoing similar operations, other monkeys found their social status plummet immediately when reintroduced to their group. They were treated like outcasts, attacked and forced to leave (Gazzaniga, Ivry, & Mangun, 1998).

When frontal lobe lobotomies were performed on humans, anxieties, compulsions, and obsessions decreased as in the monkeys, but personalities changed differently, as reported in the previous chapter. A major side effect of lesions to the orbitofrontal cortex was their detrimental impact on social interactions, as when Gage became rude, belligerent, and quarrelsome. Researchers later found that people whose orbitofrontal cortex is damaged by disease or accident still accurately assess the significance of particular situations, but only in a *theoretical* sense; they do not behave accordingly. For example, Carlson (1995) reports on research conducted by Eslinger and Damasio, which found that removal of a benign tumor caused bilateral damage to the orbitofrontal cortex. Surprisingly, the patient displayed excellent social judgment, and when asked to state solutions to moral, ethical, or practical situations, he gave sensible answers and justified them with carefully reasoned logic. He failed, however, to apply his own reasoning to his actions. He wasted the family savings on investments his wife urged him not to make. He moved from one job to another because he was irresponsible. He spent as much time deciding trivial matters—such as what to prepare for dinner—as he did on matters impacting his job and his family. As Eslinger and Damasio put it: "He had learned and used normal patterns of social behavior before his brain lesion, and although he could recall such patterns when he was questioned about their applicability, *real-life situations failed to evoke them"* (Carlson, 1985, p. 302).

Carlson concludes that the orbitofrontal cortex was not directly involved in making judgments and conclusions about events—"these occur elsewhere in the brain," he states; the orbitofrontal cortex is critical for "translating these judgments into appropriate feelings and behaviors" (p. 302). Consequently, perceiving the meaning of social situations involves analysis of sensory stimuli, as well as experiences, memories, inferences, and judgments. Carlson believes that the skills involved in social situations include some of the most complex ones we possess.

Functions of the Social Learning System

Neurobiologists believe that human social systems reflect—at the deepest level—those of other mammals studied extensively. The tendency to associate, establish links, live side by side, and cooperate is an essential characteristic of humans, as well as other mammals (Panksepp, 1998). Consequently, even when we place a high value on *independence, interdependence* is a natural human trait (Covey, 1989). For example, interdependence that humans call *love* focuses on maternal and paternal bonding, relationships between two people ("dyadic" relationships), and the need for group affiliation, altruism, and reciprocal altruism. At various times, each of these characteristics reveals a negative side: panic and separation distress, grief, sorrow, isolation, and loneliness. Similarly, although play and joy serve key roles in bonding relationships at all ages, they, too, have a flip side: episodes of conflict.

At least two social subsystems, composed of many lesser subsystems, are involved with the brain's social system. The first specializes in dyadic relation-ships—this one is ready to go at birth—and the second specializes in group rela-tionships—which take a little longer to assemble (Harris, 1998). Although serving different purposes, both subsystems develop from mother/child relationships within the context of family, peer groups, and community.

Maternal Nurturance and Bonding

Maternal bonding depends on physiological and hormonal changes in the mother's brain and body, such as the elevation of estrogen during the last few days of preg-nancy, that prompt an increase of oxytocin and oxytocin receptors (Harris, 1998). Oxytocin—a brain chemical that evolved to influence female sexual behavior—helps deliver mammalian babies by promoting uterine contractions and triggering milk letdown from mammary tissues. It also facilitates maternal moods and actions, including a sense of altruism, in new mothers.

Steven Pinker, a cognitive neuroscientist and the author of *The Language Instinct* (1994) and *How the Mind Works* (1997), says that the altruism-causing gene evolved to benefit another person at a cost to himself. Parenting is a good example, because the feeling of altruism motivates behavior like nurturing, feeding, and pro-tecting that benefit children. In everyday language, altruistic acts are called *love*—feelings of pleasure in other people's well-being and pain in their harm.

Babies depend on getting their physical needs met, receiving sensory stimula-tion, being talked to, and receiving love and support from caretakers. When fathers assume these care-giving roles, bonding between baby and father strengthens. These dyadic needs are surprisingly similar in both children and adults; thus, as baby responds to mother's attentions, mother is rewarded and feels fulfilled. If no reciprocal bonds exist, a baby's or child's distress cries for support, love, and caring may only irritate the parent and may result in child abuse or neglect, producing feel-ings of isolation, chronic insecurity, and neediness or emptiness for the child. How parents or caregivers introduce babies to their contextual world of family and nurture them, therefore, has great bearing on the children's subsequent relationships.

The absence of bonding drives children to cling to adults, avoid social interactions, or chronically disrupt social interactions of others. Research suggests that children deprived of strong bonding relationships feel rebuffed so frequently that they detach from emotional desires, build high levels of mistrust, and no longer reach out to others (Panksepp, 1998). Conversely, securely "attached" children feel confident their needs will be met, and they tend to be outgoing, optimistic, and enthusiastic about life. Mothers' altruism, therefore, prompts reciprocal altruism in children.

Altruistic nurturing during the first few weeks and months of a baby's life not only establishes the maternal bond, it also establishes neural circuits in the baby's brain for face and voice identification. These circuits help the baby's brain select and report on social events quickly and accurately to ensure the baby's safety and survival (Brothers, 1997; Donald, 1991; Jackendoff, 1994).

Face Recognition

Human babies direct their gaze toward sights and sounds—especially human faces—to receive a steady stream of social stimulation. This is necessary for babies to construct neural cell assemblies for interpretation of social situations (Brothers, 1997). For example, 7- to 11-week-old infants tend to shift their gaze to the expressive movements in the regions around the eyes when adults talk. From these observations, Leslie Brothers, clinical professor of psychiatry, UCLA School of Medicine, concludes that a baby's natural attention to expressive faces and voices forms the developmental building blocks that lead to the concept of person, the understanding of expressive communication, and the ability to participate in conversation.

Happy, pleasant faces tend to trigger spontaneous cooing and smiles associated with endorphines in the baby's brain, whereas furrowed brows and angry faces tend to stimulate the production of stress chemicals like cortisol. Babies quickly begin to imitate facial expressions that build their own neural pathways. If mother looks sad, whines, and cries easily when slightly upset, baby learns to look sad, whine, and cry. If mother smiles and laughs readily at slight difficulties, baby learns to take difficulties in stride.

Voice Recognition

Imitation of what babies hear is equally powerful. To illustrate its effects, parent and child can often sound so much alike that callers may not recognize who is speaking on the telephone. Therefore, voice quality, as well as language expression, become established early.

The auditory system divides incoming signals into what the speaker is saying (the linguistic system), who the speaker is (voice recognition), and the speaker's emotional tone. These divisions are needed to determine whether the person speaking is friendly, threatening, indifferent, surprised, frightened, or experiencing some other emotion that may help or harm (Jackendoff, 1994).

Even with attempts to conceal intentions by masking voice qualities and facial expressions, people constantly signal emotional tone consciously or unconsciously, as the brain converts emotion into motor patterns—smiles, frowns, raising of the eyebrows, openness or aggressiveness or sensuality in the posture, and so forth (Jackendoff, 1994). Young babies develop skills from birth to interpret these signals; and the patterns soon figure prominently into their ability to establish bonds of kinship, group membership, and a sense of trust and honesty.

Social Trust and Mistrust

Face and voice-recognition skills play key roles in identifying people who use sham emotions as a pretense to be generous, guilty, sympathetic, or appreciative. Seeing through these shams seems to be an ability that evolved genetically in humans. Children are vigilant for sham emotions and put their trust in involuntary physiological giveaways, whereas adults can often be fooled. Because babies develop *trust* and *mistrust* modules to discriminate between real and sham emotions, many children easily detect pretense in parents and teachers. Once mistrust sets in, it takes a great deal to overcome it (Pinker, 1997). Honesty in displaying emotions may indeed be the best policy.

As Stephen Covey (1989) stated in *The Seven Habits of Highly Effective People:*

The most important ingredient we put into any relationship is not what we say or what we do, but what we are. And if our words and our actions come from superficial human relations techniques . . . rather than from our own inner core . . . , others will sense that duplicity. We simply won't be able to create and sustain the foundation necessary for effective interdependence. (p. 187)

One-on-one family relationships, like dyadic mother/child bonding, have this same need for authenticity—that is, a congruence between a person's body language and what she says.

Dyadic Family Relationships

Children and adults develop dyadic relationships within the context of the family structure that consist largely in knowing how to behave in the presence of other people. Through family interactions, children learn to socialize; they learn to understand how others feel, and they learn to use their actions to shape and manage the feelings of others. Therein lies considerable interdependence of the emotional and social learning systems.

In *Emotional Intelligence*, Daniel Goleman (1995) writes that being able to manage emotions in someone else and set the emotional or feeling tone of an interaction is an art. It is, he says, the core of handling relationships and a sign of dominance at a deep and intimate level; it means driving the emotional state of the other person. This power to determine emotion is not seen as a manipulative force but as a process that coordinates, or entrains, one person's biological rhythms with those of another. As noted earlier, it generally occurs naturally as when walking briskly with someone and noticing that your steps are in rhythm with the other person's.

Goleman (1995) suggests that children *learn* to be sensitive, to know how someone else is feeling, and to use their social learning system to act in ways that further shape those feelings. Clearly, some children demonstrate higher aptitude than others for social-emotional entrainment, for understanding how others feel, and for purposefully acting in ways that influence the positive outcome of situations. These children generally engender smiles and positive strokes in return. Further, their peers like them better than children who tend to be sullen or angry, or who fail to express an understanding of how others feel.

Consequently, children who understand emotions—theirs and those of their peers—have more positive peer relations. They tend to interact more successfully when a friend gets angry with them, and they can talk about their own emotions; this process helps them negotiate disputes with friends. Children who are sad or angry and sit on the sidelines of the group or querulously huff around the room are less likely to see and attend to the emotional needs of others (Denham, 1998). Overall, happy children fare well, and angry children fare worse in group settings.

One way to foster social learning is to ask questions that help children consider how others feel in various situations and then formulate meaningful responses. For example, when Diane Sawyer interviewed the mother of quintuplets on television, Sawyer asked how the parents taught their six 5-year-olds to be so thoughtful of one another. The young mother explained that after playing a game, she asked her children—whether winners or losers—to consider how the others felt. Asking them to reflect on the winner/loser roles, she believed, helped them see the nuances of playing games from various perspectives. Also, each of the children had a rotating household responsibility, from setting the table to cleaning the toilet; and their weekly responsibility helped them take care of their belongings and each other.

Many children have little to no intimate nurturing within their family relationships, and they come to school quite needy. Conversation in their families tends to be one-sided utilitarian commands, rather than meaningful dialogue: "Pick up your clothes." "Shut the door." "Eat your supper." "Do your homework." "Go to bed." The need for intimacy, therefore, is left unsatisfied; and such children can feel isolated and emotionally alone in the midst of others unless they have siblings, peers, or teachers who provide the closeness so desired.

Peer Relationships

As noted earlier, some scientists suggest that personality is a mix of genetics and environmental rearing, with genetics playing a minor role. If that theory is true, what influences shape personality? Judith Harris suggests in her 1998 book *The Nurture Assumption* that parental influence is minimal compared to peer and sibling influence. Her theory states that, within that portion outside the realm of parental influence, social learning and personality are, to a large extent, what children do to themselves.

Social learning is the development of skills and understanding about self, others, and the environment as a result of interactions. It is learning to recognize how others feel and then enjoying, enhancing, or modifying those feelings for the sake of the social situation. Therefore, moving into peer relationships during the developmental years is a major transition for many children. Also, their social competence—especially the management of emotional arousal that accompanies social interactions—is fundamental for their growing ability to interact with and form relationships with others at school (Saarni, cited in Denham, 1998).

If a child's social reactions are, for the most part, "constructed" in response to peer and sibling interactions, as Harris (1998) believes, then school cultures are powerful forces in the development of how children interpret and respond to situations and circumstances. Thus, classroom and school norms take on extremely important roles regarding the development of socially acceptable behavior and in learning how to resolve conflicts.

The Chemistry of Friendship

It seems that friendships and social learning are forged by the same chemical systems that mediate maternal and sexual urges. That is, children and adults like to spend time with others whose presence increases their brain oxytocin and opioid activities. Once these chemicals associate with particular people, the same chemicals tend to be triggered whenever those persons are close by. School, therefore, needs to be a place where children get to know one another at a deep level, a place where they feel good in the company of their teachers and classmates.

Panksepp (1998) hypothesizes that one reason certain people become addicted to external opiates (i.e., alkaloids, such as morphine and heroin, that can bind to opiate receptors) is that these opiates are able to artificially induce feelings of gratification. These feelings are similar to those normally achieved by the socially induced release of endogenous opioids, such as endorphins and enkephalins, when in the company of supportive friends. Friendship is so powerful that investigators can increase opiate consumption in experimental animals simply by isolating them from the companionship of others. Interestingly, opiate addiction in humans is most common in environments where social isolation and alienation are endemic.

Unfortunately, as previously indicated, social isolation often occurs in the midst of others. It is sad to realize that children can attend the same classes five days a week for 10 months and never really know their classmates well enough to think of them as trusted friends. Because children feel better about those they know, trust, and like than they do about strangers, teachers are wise to consider classroom activities that trigger "feel good" brain chemicals. As well, teachers need to devise activities that etch the faces, voices, and behavior of *pleasant people* in memory (Panksepp, 1998). From a succession of experiences that build a feeling of community, a sense of belonging, or "groupness," can emerge, where no one feels isolated.

Groupness

A school must be a community of learners with well-established cultural patterns, moral consensus, and rituals designed to embrace each student into group membership; it cannot be just a place where students are obligated to spend time. This is especially critical because school enrollment far surpasses the ideal human group size of 155 to 175 (Donald, 1991), and middle and high school students often move from one class to the next with little opportunity for establishing meaningful group membership in individual classes. For those groups of students where socially appropriate membership is out of reach, primitive instincts and drives tend to surface and produce aggression and other undesirable behaviors. Without question, social messages of the school community feed the construction of social-emotional development, and they underscore the need for school cultures to be purposefully planned, rather than allowed to develop in a haphazard fashion (Griffiths, 1997).

Youngsters who participate in street gangs and extracurricular clubs do so based on the recognition of basic similarities (we are alike in some way) or of shared fate (we are all in the same boat) (Harris, 1998). In school settings when student "stars" shun those not like them, trouble brews until it erupts in some unfortunate way. Perhaps the worst case was in Littleton, Colorado, where two disenfranchised youths at Columbine High School felt isolated from the mainstream and deliberately shot and killed classmates before killing themselves.

The Columbine tragedy and other school shootings underscore the fact that each social group has a code of conduct that is understood by all its members; people in the group know implicitly or explicitly that their code does not necessarily apply to other groups, which have their own codes. A group's patterns of conduct are internally constructed, much like language is internally constructed from the culture (Jackendoff, 1994). Also, groups have their own cultural "values," and any group admires those who adopt those values by dishing out respect and praise. Those who violate group values receive a strong dose of scorn and "discipline" consistent with the group's culture (Wright, 1994).

Whoever seeks group membership must change his behavior to match whatever is compatible with the group. When someone does not change his behavior, laughter is the group's favorite weapon; it is used around the world to keep nonconformers in line. Those for whom laughter alone does not work—those who don't know what they are doing wrong or who will not or cannot conform—suffer a worse fate: They are expelled from the group (Harris, 1998).

Reciprocal Altruism

As implied earlier in the chapter, *liking* is motivated by an emotion that initiates and maintains an altruistic partnership; *reciprocal altruism* is a willingness to offer someone a favor who appears willing to offer favors in return. This reciprocal behavior is seen when we are nice to people we like, and they are nice to us. We don't always expect something in return, but if nothing ever comes back, the desire to be altruistic fades. Friendship is built on reciprocal altruism.

In most cultures, reciprocal altruism tends to exert some pressure toward friendliness, as well as generosity and honesty within the group (Wright, 1994). Reciprocal altruism and adhering to the group's code of conduct mean having friends—even if those friends engage in antisocial behaviors. Unfortunately, legions of youth today value status and "respect" of peers within counterproductive groups (like many gangs), because within the group, friends help each other. "This may seem obvious," wrote Robert Wright (1994) in *The Moral Animal: Why We Are the Way We Are.* "What, after all, are friends for?" (p. 249). Without bonding or belonging to a group that practices productive reciprocal altruism in school settings, children and adolescents can quickly experience a sense of isolation, loneliness, and even panic. These young people may turn to reciprocal altruism outside the school setting, to their detriment and the detriment of society.

Panic and Separation Distress

Separation distress is the flip side of attachment and bonding, but—surprisingly—these feelings appear to be mediated by the same neurochemicals: dopamine, phenethylamine, opioids, oxytocin, acetylcholine, serotonin, and other molecules of the social-emotional system. For example, low levels of opioids and high levels of oxytocin alleviate grief and loneliness whereas the reverse levels associate with the pain of separation distress and panic.

The panic or distress system serves as a barometer for measuring levels of social support. When social contact is lost, painful feelings of separation, such as loneliness, childhood depression, panic attacks, and despair, motivate attempts to reestablish contact and care (Panksepp, 1998). When people suffer panic attacks, they feel as if their center of comfort and stability has been abruptly removed. This feeling of panic prompts them to solicit help and social support—often by whining, crying, and striking out. When once again in the midst of friendly company or the ones they love, they experience a sense of calm and reassurance that floods the brain and body.

Separation distress due to social loss is the major precipitating factor for depression in humans—particularly when children are separated from their parents through abandonment, divorce, or death. During times of separation, a stress chemical called CRF (corticotrophin-releasing factor from the cortex) and adrenaline increase, and norepinephrine, serotonin, and certain dopamine reserves decrease. As a result, the victim is pushed into a depressed state accompanied by loneliness and grief (Panksepp, 1998). Children may protest the separation by their vocalizations of distress (crying, angry outbursts, etc.) and subsequent despair, but so long as the loss is felt, the brain's neurochemistry reacts.

Although separation distress research has primarily focused on animals deprived of maternal nurturing, it may be hypothesized that humans experience separation distress when separated from experiences that provide a sense of well-being. For example, many kinds of losses could create a sense of separation from the thing that brings comfort: loss of an ability through illness or accident, loss of perceived esteem in the eyes of others within one's social group, or loss of a basketball victory when it seemed assured. Without question, the ability to experience separation distress when isolated from social support is the direct opposite of neurochemically mediated comfort when social contacts are reestablished.

Gentle touch can often help restore the brain's antidistress neurochemicals. Pleasant touch, hugs, and stroking appear to activate endogenous opioid systems that release low levels of opioids, reinforcing social bonds of those we enjoy (Panksepp, 1998). Indeed, during the evolutionary process, the pleasure of touch may have established a neural framework for the emergence of play; and without it, a person may suffer extreme sense of isolation and loneliness.

Isolation and Loneliness

Isolation is pervasive in our culture. Long distances often separate relatives and prevent children from enjoying close relationships with extended family members. The demise of neighborhood togetherness where, as in the African proverb, "the whole village raises its children," and limited attendance at church, synagogue, or mosque functions further rob children of opportunities for closeness outside the home and school. To make matters worse, school curricula tend to be impersonal unless teachers deliberately develop opportunities for establishing deep friendships within learning communities. Without positive friendships, a yearning for closeness and a sense of community elevates the sense of isolation and fosters the growing trend in gang and cult membership. This escalation seems to occur because gang leaders tend to play paternal roles that emulate "family" relationships.

Researchers have noted low levels of serotonin and increased forms of aggression in children who experience prolonged social isolation or hunger (Panksepp, 1998). Teachers need to be aware of this finding, because punishment for chronically disruptive schoolchildren often includes isolation from their peers, restriction from participating in field trips and class parties, and other forms of isolation. Also, parents often restrict children to their room for long periods of isolation. This practice of isolating children needs to be seriously reconsidered, because it is an unproductive practice in the long run. It tends to increase all forms of aggression, because it lowers serotonin levels. Further, social isolation encourages children to "blame" others for their misfortune; and this reproach leads to subsequently higher levels of aggression, stronger prejudices against those blamed, and failure to take responsibility for their own behaviors (Panksepp).

Without question, gang membership fulfills the need for intimacy; a disenfranchised student can go into a gang and suddenly be part of an intimate group. Anything that promotes a sense of intimacy, community, and connection can be healing, because it relieves that gnawing sense of loneliness. Achieving a sense of belonging, however, may be detrimental to the individual and society when antisocial behavior generates alienation by socially conscious citizens in school settings and the larger community (Ford, 1992). Consequently, major group alienation tends to mirror the loss of love that gang members often feel when their biological families provide limited bonding. Although the person may feel acceptance within the gang or cult, that membership ultimately fails as a social-emotional elixir because it cannot produce the sense of unconditional acceptance and love so desperately desired from family members, school associations, or society at large.

Studies of adults have shown that people who feel isolated—who do not feel a real sense of intimate connection with other people—have three to five times the mortality rate from cardiovascular disease and all other causes, when compared to people who do not feel isolated (Ornish, 1993). Similar studies have not been conducted with children and youth; however, observations suggest that the large number of students identified for "alternative education" programs because of emotional disturbances or behavior disorders suffer from their unmet psychological needs for love and belonging. The questions are: Do teachers consciously nurture students to ensure that every child has an adult who cares about him or her? Do teachers ensure that all children have a positive peer group to support them?

According to Panksepp (1998), when those we love disappear or the love we seek is never forthcoming,

> we find ourselves plunged into one of the deepest and most troubling emotional pains of which we, as social creatures, are capable. In everyday language, this feeling is called sorrow or grief, and it can verge on panic in its most intense and precipitous forms. At a less acute but more persistent level, the same essential feeling is called loneliness or sadness. (p. 261)

Children suffering a sense of isolation and loneliness tend to withdraw, appear depressed, and turn away from opportunities to engage in rough and tumble play.

Play

In the animal world, mammals—other than humans—become rather self-sufficient shortly after weaning, because they are expected to get serious about food, shelter, and predators shortly after birth. Human babies, by contrast, are totally dependent for several years during a long, sheltered childhood. Without having to worry about survival needs, human babies and children are free to explore possible solutions to real or pretend problems through play, games, and simple contests. "But how does a brain unconsciously generate the requisite emotional arousal without the presence of real danger or opportunity?" asked Robert Sylwester (2000), author of *A Celebration of Neurons* (1995) and *A Biological Brain in a Cultural Classroom* (2000). He then answered his rhetorical question by stating that good games of pretend extend consciousness and foster motor, language, and social learning; they develop easily and without much adult instruction as emotional arousal is sparked. In turn, emotional arousal activates attention, problem solving, and behavior response systems. Play, therefore, is essential for learning—especially play with others.

Researchers have found that playfulness is seriously restricted when a person feels socially isolated. After several days of isolation, for example, young monkeys and chimps exhibit relatively little play when reunited with their friends. Rather, they become despondent until their needs for social warmth, support, and affiliation are fulfilled. When confidence is restored, carefree playfulness returns (Panksepp, 1998).

Adolescents in classes for chronically disruptive youth generally display an unusually limited ability to engage in playful social interactions while displaying an unusually high propensity for lethargy intermixed with outbursts of anger. These behaviors tend to reflect distress cries for unconditional love and a strong need for social warmth and support before the thought of play can be entertained—whether that play is exploratory/sensorimotor play, functional play, constructive play, dramatic/symbolic play, games-with-rules play, or rough-and-tumble play. Lack of interest in play may result from events that evoke negative emotional states, such as fear, anger, and separation distress. Once humans are healthy and feel good, play becomes an appealing psychobehavioral option. When they feel bad, it is not (Panksepp, 1998).

Unfortunately, students who seldom engage in play may be less effective in competitive encounters later in life because they have failed to learn certain skills, such as various competitive and noncompetitive social interpretations that influence bonding, social cooperation, social ranking, leadership, and communication. Also, limited playfulness can hamper the development of physical fitness, cognitive abilities, skillful tool use, and the ability to innovate through creative thinking. Ample doses of play throughout life, however, can inoculate people against social stress in future adult competitive encounters. Play can also facilitate social attractiveness. On the dark side, it can help refine deceptive skills and the ability to create false impressions for achieving a competitive edge (Panksepp, 1998).

Play and Learning. Apparently, the brain's play system learns rapidly early in life; witness a baby smile and giggle at an adult's wiggling finger that signals "tickletime." Children learn more rapidly when they have fun, and there is scientific research to support this assumption (Dunn & Dunn, 1993). Without question, learning experiences that look like play certainly make learning more fun and less tedious than basic work on difficult information.

Location of Play in the Brain. The neocortex is not essential for play, but play mentally programs playful interactions in the neocortex (Panksepp, 1998). Other brain structures, however, figure prominently in the play circuit, including neurons that project from the spinal cord into the limbs and other neurons that project from the thalamus to the parietal lobes. Of course, the vestibular, cerebellar, and basal ganglia systems control movement that is important in play.

Chemicals of Play. In play, if one mammal tends to be a consistent "winner" and the other a consistent "loser," the first may develop increased levels of opioids, such as endogenous morphine, that increase aggressiveness and bullying tendencies. As a result, the second player generally feels psychologically weaker, withdraws, and begins to ignore advances for play by the first (Panksepp, 1998). The educational practice of consistently pairing a strong student with a weak student is fine so long as the weak student has opportunities to demonstrate strengths in other circumstances.

When winning and losing are balanced, play and laughter tend to be a "neurotonic" for the relief of stress and other negative emotions of the play partners. This may be the result of keeping opioid production low because high levels reduce all social behaviors, including play. Panksepp (1998) finds that high levels of oxytocin and CRF also reduce the desire to play, whereas dopamine neurons are especially active during play. In the midst of intensive or prolonged play, children may gradually reach a point where fun turns to anger, fear, or separation distress as play continues to produce ongoing winners and losers. Further, some forms of play can create sexual arousal that produces its own kinds of fear and confusion. At the point when play takes a negative turn, the playful mood subsides as chemical production in the brain shifts.

Play and Attention. Attention deficit hyperactivity disorders (ADHD), impulse-control disorders (impulsiveness), and rapid shifting from one activity to another—all these attentional difficulties seem to be related to uncontained and unfocused playful tendencies. Panksepp (1998) reports his concern about the use of medications to control playfulness:

Medications that are used to treat the disorder [ADHD]—psychostimulants such as methylphenidate (i.e., Ritalin ©) and amphetamines—are all very effective in reducing playfulness in animals. . . . Moreover, parents of hyperkinetic children often complain that one of the undesirable side effects of such medications is the reduced playfulness of their children. . . . Obviously, it is essential to maintain attention to academic matters in the classroom, but is it appropriate to induce compliance in children through pharmacological means? (p. 297)

At the very least, more benign interventions should be attempted first, such as provision of abundant RAT [rough and tumble play] activity early in the morning prior to classes. This is especially important in light of the possibility that such drugs can produce long-lasting changes in the responsivity of brain catecholamine systems, as is seen in the psychostimulant-induced sensitization phenomenon [whereby] . . . the nervous system becomes sensitized to psychostimulants, and animal research indicates that such modifications of the nervous system can be permanent. (p. 320)

Because play generates powerful positive emotional states, teachers may wish to make difficult material playful, particularly for children who are generally active or somewhat hyperactive (Dunn & Dunn, 1992, 1993). The extent of instructional play used in the school setting, however, is greatly influenced by the community and school cultures that either endorse or denounce it.

Social Culture

Anthropologists have seen recurring patterns in the structure of family, friendship, politics, courtship, and morality from prehistoric times to the present throughout various cultures, despite their differences (Wright, 1994). According to Robert Wright, senior editor for *The New Republic*, anthropologists believe that biology explains

why people in all cultures worry about social status . . . ; why people in all cultures not only gossip, but gossip about the same kinds of things; why in all cultures men and women seem different in a few basic ways; why people everywhere feel guilt, and feel it in broadly predictable circumstances; shy people everywhere have a deep sense of justice, so that the axioms "One good turn deserves another" and " An eye for an eye, a tooth for a tooth" shape human life everywhere on this planet. (pp. 7–8)

Wright (1994) goes on to say that children in diverse cultures lower their heads in self-abasement after losing a fight, and that "people in all cultures feel pride upon social success, embarrassment, even shame, . . . failure, and, at times, anxiety pending these outcomes" (p. 242). Although human genes that pertain to social learning appear to be more similar than different from culture to culture, Ruth Benedict (1934) pointed out some years ago that what is considered abnormal or deviant in one culture may be considered normal or even virtuous in another.

Cultural Genes

Children are not *taught* cultural patterns and social understandings through the transmission of rules; they absorb, interpret, and act out what they self-construct, based on input received from all of culture (Jackendoff, 1994). "All of culture" includes television, music, and movies whose messages often conflict with family and community values. Thus, children and youth may experience internal turmoil regarding what principles, behaviors, religious beliefs, and language patterns to follow—those they observe through the mass media or those they see exhibited by their family members or those espoused at school.

Richard Dawkins (1976/1989), author of *The Selfish Gene*, coined the word *meme* (rhymes with *gene*) to convey the concept of cultural transmission of tunes, religious beliefs, ideas, catch-phrases, clothes fashions, ways of making pots or of building arches, and most things transmitted or perhaps reproduced via culture. He says that just as "genes propagate themselves in the gene pool by leaping from body to body via sperms or eggs, memes propagate themselves in the meme pool by leaping from brain to brain via a process which, in the broad sense, can be called imitation" (p. 186).

Dawkins (1976/1989) believes that what is most unusual about humans can be shown by their culture and how it is transmitted or reproduced. Children learn partly by observing examples of family members, but they assimilate family values together with what they observe in society; then they internally construct the patterns of culture and social understanding in their own minds. Thus, sensory input from all aspects of society is critically important in what children believe and how children act. Nonetheless, sensory input alone does not constitute a meme unit (Blackmore, 1999).

Dawkins (1976/1989) said that memes pass on culture from generation to generation, but a more radical view is that culture actually changes the gene structure of individuals. In *Origins of the Modern Mind*, Merlin Donald (1991) states:

> Cultures restructure the mind, not only in terms of its specific contents, which are obviously culture-bound, but also in terms of its fundamental

neurological organization. . . . Culture can literally reconfigure the use patterns of the brain; and it is probably a safe inference from our current knowledge of cerebral plasticity that those patterns of use determine much about how the exceptionally plastic human central nervous system is ultimately organized, in terms of cognitive structure. (p. 14)

Donald (1991) is not alone in his analysis that society alters genes. Steve Jones (1994), professor of genetics and head of the Galton Laboratories at University College, London, believes that since modern humans first evolved, society has driven gene configuration. He believes that today's advances in complex technologies are creating an evolutionary shift with biological consequences that will last for thousands of years.

If Merlin Donald and Steve Jones are correct, perhaps society is creating or dramatically contributing to the hyperactivity in many children. With the discovery that humans have between 30,000 and 40,000 genes—only about 10,000 more genes than a worm—rather than the 100,000 or so anticipated, the role of nurture (including culture) in determining human behavior appears more significant than nature (Orr, 2001).

Because social learning can be automatic or intentional—based on Dawkins's memetic assumptions—we must consider the effect of media on human gene configuration for future generations. For example, social learning is automatic or without conscious effort when toddlers learn a language or develop prejudices and beliefs from family members; learning results from intentional input when the media desensitize children to the loss of life from frequent explicit scenes of violence on television. What the media portray influences in some way how the brain evolves because mass media are a part of culture. Out of his great concern for what children construct mentally, Amitai Etzioni, author of *The Spirit of Community*, coined the word *communitarianism* to explain why "strong rights presume strong responsibilities" from citizens of a given culture (cited in Berreth & Scherer, 1993, p. 12). He says that about half the families in the United States "no longer see it as their duty to pass along values from generation to generation." If schools fail to assume this responsibility, he believes, "then just as we have adults who are deficient in writing and science, we will find that adults won't have the character and the values needed to be decent members of the community or decent employees or decent soldiers" (p. 12).

Character

Character is the human quality that emerges from social learning. According to Pinker (1997), how we choose to behave is a complex interaction among many influences:

> Our genes.
> Our family rearing.
> Our culture and our interpretation of it that organizes our neural networks.
> The biochemical state of our brains at any one time.
> The way society has treated us.
> Incoming stimuli and circumstances.

We are all capable of ugly acts against one another, but we are also capable of love, friendship, cooperation, a sense of fairness, and an ability to predict the consequences of our actions.

Brain chemistries that promote pleasure and family values are able to dramatically reduce irritability and aggressiveness in societies (Panksepp, 1998). Human societies tend to be least aggressive where physical closeness, touching, and the free flow of intimacy exist. For instance, in societies where adults exhibit high levels of physical affection toward infants, children, and each other, adult physical violence is generally low, because affection increases both opioids and oxytocin—powerful antiaggressive molecules. Societies low in physical affection and high in punishment tend to be more violent. Pinker (1997) believes that "the theory of a module-packed mind allows both for innate motives that lead to evil acts and for innate motives that can avert them" (p. 51). This is neither a recent nor a unique discovery, because most major religions observe that mental life and character are often a struggle between desire and conscience. Complicated negotiations go on inside the head, with one module subverting another. Conflicts are a human universal, but so are efforts to reduce them. "The different parts of the mind struggle to engage or disengage the clutch pedal of behavior," Pinker concludes, "so bad thoughts do not always cause bad deeds" (pp. 53, 517–518).

Some students whose sense of belonging has been warped early in life need considerable help in learning to engage in positive social behavior. They seem not to have developed functional brain modules that support an internalized moral philosophy and a code of ethics, or those functional modules are weak and easily defeated by primitive urges during a modular battle (Jackendoff, 1994).

Psychiatrist Robert Cloninger, Washington University Medical School in St. Louis, studied character traits in 1,019 people from age 18 to 99, and found that those in middle and older age ranges generally improved their relationship behaviors (cited in Hamer & Copeland, 1998, pp. 292–294). He reported that people generally become more willing to treat others fairly and with kindness and compassion as they get older; they tend to become more spiritual; they also express warmth, altruism, positive emotions, and openness of feelings. He found that middle- and older-aged people are relatively more intimate, friendly, generous, and concerned for the welfare of others; they are more optimistic about life and more likely to experience positive emotions such as love and happiness; and they are more open to their own inner feelings and emotions than during their earlier years. Thus, older teachers *may* be the more compassionate teachers and better able to resolve social conflicts at school. On the other hand, if older teachers have developed habitual neuro "wiring" patterns that are detrimental to children, then their character changes may be too limited for positive benefit.

Social Conflict

Contrary to Oscar Wilde's admonition that "nothing worth knowing can be taught," skills for resolving conflicts peacefully are a clear exception. Such skills are solely needed in the United States, where personal conflicts often end in assault— or worse, murder. By the year 2010, the U.S. Census Bureau expects the population of males between the ages of 15 and 19 to reach a whopping 11.5 million (McNulty, 1995). Since the 14- to 24-year-old age group is responsible for the largest portion of all violent crimes in America, population increases raise serious social concerns (U.S. Department of Justice, 1996, 2001). For example, in 1999, 2.5 million persons under the age of 18 were arrested for serious offenses, property crimes, and other crimes, including arson, larceny-theft, drug abuse violations, disorderly conduct, liquor law violations, vandalism, burglary, aggravated assault, other assaults, and motor vehicle theft. Sex offenses account for 16,600 arrests (National Center for Juvenile Justice, 2000).

The number of delinquency cases in the United States increased 30 percent from 1988 to 1997, with nearly 6 percent of the acts being committed by children

10 years of age (Wilson, 2000). The number of 13- to 15-year-olds arrested for murder jumped from 390 in 1982 to 740 ten years later (McNulty, 1995). Juvenile arrests for heroin and cocaine rose more than 700 percent between 1980 and 1990, with the rate of increase for African American teenagers increasing 2,000 percent (DiIulio, 1994).

According to 1999 figures, aggravated assault committed by juveniles decreased after an all-time high in 1994 (OJJDP [Office of Juvenile Justice and Delinquency Prevention], 2000). Nonetheless, this slight decrease by 1999 fails to quell concern because the "good news" reveals a 48-percent increase in aggravated assault arrests for youths ages 15 to 17 compared to the 1980 data. During the 1996-97 academic year, 77 percent of high school principals in the United States reported to the police at least one incident of crime/violence (theft, vandalism, fights, or assaults without a weapon); and the homicide rate among 14- to 17-year-olds was 19.8 per 100,000 persons in this age range (Violence Institute, 2001). Lack of civility and peaceful conflict resolution at the kinship level resulted in 99,776 arrests across ages for offenses against the family and children in 1998. At least 46,924 children under age 15 were arrested as runaways, with 1,623 of these under the age of 10.

Children who feel loved, valued, and important do not run away or commit crimes against themselves or others; yet carrying a weapon to school continues to be a significant problem. Further, in 1998, a total of 84 children under age 10 were charged with forcible rape, and 51,360 youngsters under the age of 18 (5 of whom were between the ages of 5 and 9) committed suicide—the ultimate violent act against one's self and the most dramatic indicator of emotional-social pain, isolation, and loneliness (OJJDP, 2000).

Deterrents such as reduced or lost privileges, school suspensions, expulsions, or incarceration may prevent the awful statistics from being higher, but these disciplinary measures have little effect on many students involved in the chain of acting-out behaviors that get them into trouble—impulsive acts that lead to aggression, hostility, and acts of violence. To prevent the cycle from getting started, we need classroom interventions specifically designed to help students control their impulsivity.

Educational Considerations

School and classroom cultures that give students opportunities to belong to meaningful groups, to have leadership experiences, to gain respect from their peers, and to participate in reciprocal altruism require purposeful planning and organization.

Thoughtful planning for the classroom culture is critical because students in each class—whether woodworking, math, history, or government—will develop an unwritten code of conduct that either supports the curriculum or undermines it. It takes masterful teachers who collaborate with students to create a social and academic code of conduct where all students achieve to their highest potential as an accepted expectation for class membership. This code must honor the need for relationship preferences and must shape character for students' individual good and for the good of the group.

When planning interactions, we must take individual differences and styles into account: Some students learn best when working with another student or in a small group; others learn best when left alone to process information in their own time in their own way, and others feel more secure and focused when working with the teacher, another adult, or other authority figure (Dunn & Dunn, 1993). Peer-interaction and cooperative-learning groups may be frustrating and anxiety producing for students who like to work alone. On the other hand, limited small-group work with peer interaction can help solo students explore alternative ways of approaching a task without feeling overwhelmed.

Students who like to interact with others often like social interactions regardless of the task. Such students generally need direction from the teacher about the subject matter and how to perform the assignment. The teacher should give clear expectations and a time limit. The following are two examples of such directions:

➤ "In the next three minutes, list as many ways as you can think of how animals move from one place to another."
➤ "As a team during Reader's and Writer's Workshop, select a fairy tale character who committed a dastardly deed—from Goldilocks, The Big Bad Wolf, Rapunzel, or the Wicked Witch from the West—and draft a 'Wanted' poster."

Without clear guidance and timelines, social students get side-tracked easily. As their on-task group skills increase, they accomplish far more than when working alone, because they are part of, rather than separate from, the sights and sounds of others—they belong to a group, provided it is a group of students with characteristics that feel comfortable and supportive. At the same time, other members of the group who prefer working alone are able to do so at their own pace without carrying the workload for those who are less task oriented.

The cyclical nature of social learning is forever evolving. It has functional and structural brain modules that evolved over time, yet we all construct our own ways of making use of them. Thus, the social learning system operates as a process of growth, improvement, and change as individuals and societies learn by doing in recursive ways, both functional and dysfunctional. For example, we intermittently search for "how things work" (functional learning) or attempt to solve social issues in simplistic ways (dysfunctional learning) (Goerner, 1994).

Thomas Lickona (1993), developmental psychologist and professor of education at State University of New York at Cortland and author of "Educating for Character: How Our Schools Can Teach Respect and Responsibility," wrote that if we are to make a lasting difference in students' character, schools need a comprehensive approach, engaging students' minds, feelings, and behavior. Educators need to ask, "Do present school practices support, neglect, or contradict the school's professed values and character education?" (p. 10). We will get nowhere with our students if we blame society for everything, he stressed. We must look at the culture of our schools and classrooms to see how we can construct communities of learners where all children are respected, have leadership opportunities, and are honored for being who they are.

Peer mentoring can provide students with practice in character ethics and leadership. As students learn new lessons, teachers can encourage them to teach the lessons to someone else. The act of peer teaching clarifies thinking and helps student-teachers notice details not previously considered. Peer mentoring gives each person the opportunity to continue skill development while developing leadership skills and self-confidence.

Keeping the Social Learning System in Balance

The brain's social learning system desires affiliation and expects to be respected and honored by members of the group. This system strives for approval by significant others and enjoys learning when engaged with those who think similarly. The *need to belong* is the greatest need of this system.

Culture is the foundation of the social learning system. From home, community, and school cultures, youngsters learn language, the preferred style of reading and writing, math symbols, beliefs, prejudices, fears, and expectations. They absorb cultural mores and create their own *vision* of what is possible for them—what they might accomplish, what they can become. Through their interactions and collaborations with friends, caring adults, and others, the vision of what is personally possible becomes clear and serves as a driving force for learning.

When the social learning system supports the individual, a sense of confidence emerges that is independent of friends' approval. A healthy social system allows friendships with persons of various ages to evolve comfortably. At the same time, recognizing others' social-emotional states is used to foster positive interactions. Working in pairs, small groups, large groups, or alone—all interactions can be pleasing, depending on the circumstances.

Some children have a low-level interest in working or playing with others, but they can do so for short periods of time. These children may have appropriate social skills, but they prefer being alone unless they can be in the company of others who think like they do. Conversely, other children lack social learning skills and withdraw from group interactions out of fear, or they overreact when included. Youngsters in these two groups are quite different even though they may prefer to work alone.

If a child functions predominantly in the social system, striving to belong may be an all-consuming endeavor. Such youngsters may lack personal identity when not in the presence of others and may fail to take responsibility for their own actions and learning. Children's dependency on what others say, do, and expect may limit their development of problem-solving skills and the ability to take constructive criticism even when gently and respectfully offered. Because they have a difficult time fulfilling their need to belong in positive ways, these youngsters may resort to misbehavior in an effort to gain attention and recognition.

All students, especially students with limited social learning skills, need teachers as *collaborators* to help them develop social strengths, such as learning how to solve problems interactively with teachers and other students. Teacher-collaborators demonstrate how to work with others by fostering shared responsibilities, healthy social interactions, strategies for interpreting social-emotional cues, and techniques for getting along. They know that specific instruction in conflict resolution, mediation, cooperative learning, and listening and speaking with good purpose are critical to the development of the social learning system.

To promote social learning, teacher-collaborators relate subject-matter content to oral communication skills. They highlight how story characters and historical figures interact with others, and they engage students in giving and critiquing oral reports. Teacher-collaborators promote the sense of belonging and a classroom code of conduct where students value learning and honor each other for their contributions to the group—whatever those contributions might be.

As suggested in the previous chapter, to deliberately model self-empowered learning, teachers—acting as mentors for students—show enthusiasm for content and a passion for learning. They interest students in learning and foster growth in each student's particular areas of interest. Teachers who honor the brain's social learning system collaborate with their students to reconsider previous knowledge and procedures and create new possibilities for everyone in the classroom community. Teacher-collaborators provide relevant learning opportunities—assignments and projects students can relate to and become invested in because teachers connect new learning with what is meaningful to students. The purpose of the mentor role is to encourage students to become all they are capable of becoming as their emotional needs are met. The purpose of the teacher-collaborator role is to build learning communities that provide respect, responsibility, and relationship—a sense of belonging, love, and connectedness for all its members.

4

The Cognitive Learning System

The cognitive learning system is the information processing system of the brain. It takes input from the outside world and all other systems, interprets that input, and guides problem solving and decision making. Because this system is directly related to academic learning, it receives the most extensive attention from educators. The cognitive system's toughest jobs include assessing emotional sensations and social situations, then acting on those assessments to keep the primal emotions under control and the need for social belonging in perspective. In similar fashion to the emotional and social systems, the cognitive learning system relies on brain chemistry for its effectiveness.

Acetylcholine, a highly pervasive neurotransmitter, mediates synaptic activity and facilitates information processing. This neurotransmitter acts on the thalamus—a walnut-sized cluster of cell bodies serving as a relay station to sort and send sensory information to the neocortex for interpretation. Acetylcholine is ubiquitous in both its presence throughout the brain and its ability to facilitate multiple functions (e.g., attention, memory, motivation, aggression) and a host of physical behaviors (e.g., biting, clenching, chewing, facial movements, arousal, drinking, vocalization).

As the last two chapters stressed, emotional and social systems have "minds of their own." Whenever these two primal systems are in turmoil, the cognitive system must spend its energy on them before it can focus on higher order thinking required for knowledge and skill acquisition. Therefore, this chapter emphasizes brain modules that directly affect academic tasks, because these modules control sensory input, consciousness, language development, attention, and memory—subsystems essential for developing academic skills.

Modules of Cognition

The cognitive learning system is composed of numerous modules throughout the brain that function collaboratively to promote learning. The largest concentration of the system's neurons resides in the neocortex, or outer "bark" of the brain. Here, the system attempts to satisfy the brain's strong need to know and its desire for authentic problem-solving challenges. In school-aged youngsters, the need to know begins with the intense desire to learn what others are learning: how to read, how to count, how to write. Novelty, movement, color, and personal interests and goals intrigue the cognitive system; it pushes for the understanding of self and others. Incorporation of these characteristics in learning tasks, therefore, makes lessons easier and more appealing.

Cognition relies on sensory modalities—smell, taste, touch, vision, hearing, and movement in particular—that function in parallel and at the same time to alert us to environmental stimuli other mental modules have filtered for our interpretation. Our self-interests, past experiences, and wide-ranging thought processes determine which sensory input to attend to and what we should do with it.

Visual and Auditory Systems

Scientists know where much of this information processing action takes place, but they are often unclear about how it occurs; whereas much is known about how neurons communicate with each other, there is little agreement on how the "mind" and "consciousness" operate. The brain's parietal, temporal, and occipital lobes, for example, are involved in auditory and visual perception. The primary visual cortex lies at the back of the occipital lobe where specific modules process input from the visual field. The primary auditory cortex is in the temporal lobes (left lobe primarily for processing languages; right primarily for environmental sounds). The primary somatosensory cortex, which lies right behind the frontal lobe's motor strip, receives and interprets information about body sensations such as touch, pressure, vibrations, and temperature. The rest of the neocortex contains association areas for each of the primary perceptual cortices; how the brain constructs these associations to create the "mind" and "consciousness" is generally unknown. Damage to any one of these areas, however, can cause impaired perceptual functioning. If children sustain damage to the visual-auditory association area, they may have difficulty reading and writing (Carlson, 1995). Without question, we can function adequately, and in some cases exceptionally well without one or two of our senses—like Helen

Keller—but sensory contact with the outside world is necessary to develop visual and auditory perceptual strengths, learn a language, and gain problem-solving skills.

In ways not yet understood, the brain "binds" sensations together so we can experience *gestalt* or whole experiences rather than unrelated bits and pieces. For example, we can see the rose, smell it, feel its texture, and hear the bee buzzing nearby all at the same time without confusing the rose with the surrounding grass, trees, or mulch, or confusing the bee's buzz with a friend's voice. Further, the brain combines all these sensations to create a whole picture of the garden. While uncertain about how the brain functions to accomplish these tasks, scientists know that information processing depends on awareness of and attention to sensory stimulation. At some level, we must be conscious of the stimulus before it can be processed.

Visual Processing. At an early age, the visual parts of the brain mysteriously dissect the visual field into shape, color, movement, location, and so on, and somehow put them all together to provide highly organized views of the world without confusing features of one object with those of another (Edelman, 1992). Much of this sorting out occurs in a knot of cells within the thalamus. Axons of these cells stretch into visual cortices of the occipital and inferior temporal lobes, where conscious interpretation occurs.

The primary visual cortex in each hemisphere consists of about 2,500 modules; each module contains about 150,000 neurons; all neurons within a single module respond to specific features, such as light frequencies, line orientation, colors, and textures (Guenther, 1998). For example, specific neurons within the "color" module respond to red, and others respond to blue, and so forth. Secondary neuron clusters process movement, form ("circle" or "square"), and whole objects ("truck" or "chair"). If damage occurs in a "movement" cluster, the person becomes unable to notice moving objects. Cars, water, and all other things in motion appear stationary. If the area that processes whole objects is damaged, the person may fail to recognize specific objects, such as his or her own fingers; this condition is called *finger agnosia* (Johnson & Myklebust, 1967).

According to leading theory on visual perception, what a person perceives is not a direct or accurate representation of reality, but a "spruced up" elaboration based on unconscious inferences built by expectations and past perceptions (Guenther, 1998). For example, two students may react quite differently to a poster showing various brain lobes and an announcement that the next thematic science unit will focus on the nervous system. A student with low reading skills and limited success in science may perceive only the portions of the poster that accentuate his weaknesses. He immediately believes that his skills are inadequate to the task, fails to see any positive aspects of the project, and responds with worry. By contrast, another student, whose background is richly endowed, may perceive abundant detail and look forward to the experience as an exciting new learning opportunity. How they receive the activities will be colored by their varying backgrounds and expectations.

Auditory Processing. The human ear and its auditory-processing modules begin developing four to five weeks after conception. During gestation, the auditory system attunes to the mother's voice and sounds in the environment. Modules in the auditory cortex process particular types of input, just like specific modules in the visual system. Some tune to brief or sustained sounds, while others process to loud or soft sounds, clicks, bursts, voices, and high and low pitches (Diamond & Hopson, 1998). If babies do not hear specific sounds early in life, neurons for processing those sounds begin functioning with alternatives that babies do hear. In essence, neurons change their "job descriptions" when the *assigned* job fails to materialize, and they begin processing sounds that occur in their environment.

To increase dendritic growth within these modules, Diamond and Hopson (1998) recommends that caregivers talk, read, and sing to babies from birth onward, and that they tell babies and toddlers the names of things, what those things are doing, and why they are doing it. Don Campbell (1997), author of *The Mozart Effect*, recommends beginning these activities during pregnancy. He reports that shortly after birth, babies turn their heads to the sound of their mother's voice more than toward other voices, and that they respond significantly more to music heard while in the womb than to unfamiliar music.

The relationship between parent talk and a child's learning was underscored by Reuven Feurestein (1980), who found that mediating the environment for children by explaining things to them helps develop reasoning and decision-making skills. For example, when asking a child to close the door, giving a reason such as *because the wind is blowing mommy's papers*, helps the child know to close the door in the future if the wind is blowing. Giving a command without explanation results in getting the door closed, but the child has no benefit from a rational explanation. Thus, mediating the environment for children teaches strategies for internal thinking, or self-talk, they will use automatically to reflect on a situation and guide their behavior.

Language

Although language is a complex and specialized skill, it is not taught like reading or telling time. Basic language develops naturally and spontaneously in every individual without conscious effort or formal instruction. Pinker (1997) believes that language development is based on genetic instructions that allow the left hemisphere to develop language as the child matures. Modules for language development, such as Wernicke's Area for understanding speech and Broca's Area for speech production, are genetically engineered to develop over time based on linguistic input.

Three things happen in children who receive extensive linguistic input: (1) their language areas develop at a more rapid rate; (2) they develop a larger vocabulary than those with limited linguistic input; and (3) they later score higher on intelligence tests (Diamond, 1998). Speech sounds begin as the grunts, cries, coos of the newborn, and graduate to trills, smacks, and clicks as a baby babbles in all languages of the world in random, nonlinear, and unintentional sounds. Babbling that matches cultural expectations is reinforced and leads to self-organization of language. When mismatches between babbling and expected sounds fail to produce reinforcement, the body learns to control what is vocalized (Goerner, 1994).

In *Magic Trees of the Mind*, Diamond and Hopson (1998) report on research conducted by Arnold Schiebel who found:

> At three to six months of age, before a baby starts talking, the dendrites on the right side of the brain are larger and "branchier" than on the left, especially in the brain areas that control sucking, swallowing, smiling, crying and other expressions, but not speech. As the baby learns to speak between [the ages of] eight and eighteen months, however, the dendritic trees in the left hemisphere (the side of the brain that controls language in most people) grow longer and branch more luxuriantly than the right. This left-side branching, Scheibel speculates, may be not the *cause* but the *response* to the baby's learning and using of words. It is therefore a classic case of dendritic growth in response to environmental stimulation—in this case, presumably, the parents' talking, singing, and reading to the baby. (p. 105)

By 10 months to 1 year, babies can make recognizable words by producing the language of their cultures. During this developmental period, children are capable of learning numerous languages, but with age, cells become "hardwired" for the language that is predominantly heard. Our facility for producing sounds not found in our native language decreases with age. For example, neurons dedicated to the sound of /j/ may switch to another sound in Hispanic children who do not hear that sound from care-givers. Vocalizations become intentional extensions of self into the cultural environment as toddlers use their language to get what they want (Goerner, 1994).

Harris found that the greatest parental contributions to children's development pertain to acquiring an initial language. When the family moves to another country, however, children learn the new language from their peers and "code-switch," using the native language at home and relying on the new language outside the home (Harris, 1998). Friends and classmates, therefore, become the most powerful force in continuing language development and usage.

Evolutionary psychologists speculate that girls demonstrate an earlier onset of language usage and fewer language deficits because our female ancestors may have developed greater temporal lobe capacity for sequential, social, and emotional aspects of language than did their male counterparts. This speculation rests on the assumption that men inhibited speech during the hunt, whereas women were free to talk while gathering plants. Today, some would say men continue to use lan-guage for two major purposes: bonding and the exchange of information related to business and sports—the modern hunt (Joseph, 1993).

Language allows humans to discuss the present, the past, and the future; to explain concrete objects; and to contemplate abstract concepts. Conversation serves as the vehicle for creating the concepts of person and society. When we have no words for feelings, thoughts, things, or ideas, we invent them and then develop vocabularies of motivation and experience to explain them (Brothers, 1997). By allowing consideration of the human condition and serving as our medium for intel-lectual exchange, language binds the social and cognitive systems in highly com-plex ways.

The role of language in the transmission or reproduction of culture is undeni-able; it cements cultural mores that endure generation after generation and plays the primary role in human interactions. However, the language children learn still depends on their local culture and social relationships, which affect how they assim-ilate and disseminate cultural mores. When students experience cultural bonding or sense of relationship with another person or group, feelings of love and belonging stimulate the social learning system toward collaborative problem solving. A sense of relationship also stimulates support for those within the culture and how individual diversity is honored, based on family and local culture standards.

Because language is culturally grounded and cultures differ in what they view as appropriate in terms of rituals, principles, and religions, language both institutes and resolves conflict. Obviously, children and adults must develop effective conflict-resolution skills if our world is to endure as a conglomerate of differing cultures. Thus, culture, language, relationship, and conflict are the major areas associated with the social learning system and its insistence on belonging.

Auditory Processing Deficit

Receiving auditory input, making some sense of it, and deciding what to do with it sounds easy, but at various places along the way, malfunctioning neurons or inappropriate chemical reactions can create hearing impairments or various learning disabilities. For example, a child may have adequate hearing but have great difficulty distinguishing the differences between sounds such as /b/, /d/, /g/, /p/, /t/ or /v/ and /f/. This is often the result of frequent middle ear infections—called *otitis media*—during the critical periods from birth to 3 years of age when language sounds begin becoming hardwired. Otitis media creates excessive fluid buildup that muffles and distorts incoming language sounds. Rather than develop discrete neural pathways for individual sounds, the child's brain tends to process all similar sounds in the same neural net. Consequently, the neurons in that net fire indiscriminately whenever any of its similar sounds are perceived. For this child, "dad," "pad," and "Tad" may all sound like the same word. When this happens, children may experience severe difficulties in learning to understand their own language, and to speak clearly, read, and spell, and they will not understand why.

Specific instruction in phonemic awareness is critical as early as possible to help children establish discrete networks before a single collective neural net becomes firmly entrenched and similar sounds are perceived as one. The child must be aware that fine discriminations are necessary to grasp the appropriate meaning of language heard. Preschool alphabet books can serve as prompts in helping children make those discriminations. Follow-up activities such as "I see something that begins with /b/. Can you guess what it is?" can be fun to play while providing necessary attention to differences in similar sounds. Without accuracy in fine discriminations, oral language difficulties soon become apparent and reading difficulties soon follow.

Language and Technology

As we use technology and telecommunications more and more, the role of language in promoting social system learning becomes more pronounced. For instance, in *Global Paradox: The Bigger the World Economy, the More Powerful Its Smallest Players*, John Nesbit (1994) discusses the rapid and widespread acceptance of the Fax machine in comparison to a slower reception of electronic mail (e-mail). Fax transmissions and personal letter writing share certain similarities, whereas e-mail requires a new telecommunications language.

Because language plays such a critical role in social learning, people personalize technology by forming online interest groups that communicate internationally via e-mail. When people can connect electronically with others who think, feel, or believe as they do, their need for belonging is addressed. Then the social learning system—for good or for ill—fosters collaborative problem solving, supports others, and honors individual diversity across the miles just as is done within family and community groups. In fact, collaboration may occur at a higher level because racial or cultural differences that may interfere because of prejudices are unknown when communicating via e-mail.

In whatever mode used, scientists believe that language holds the key to the mind just as DNA found deep within chromatin proved to hold the key to the mystery of inheritance (Brothers, 1997). Language certainly holds the key to sustaining relationships in persons across the miles. Although not yet clearly understood, language also plays a key role in consciousness.

Consciousness

Consciousness is a hotly debated phenomenon that researchers are striving to understand. Of particular interest is where it resides. Neurons are clearly the operational mechanisms that produce consciousness, so let's take a deeper look at how they function. To review, neurons have four main parts: dendrites (input fibers), the soma or cell body (computing mechanism), the nucleus (houses genetic codes in DNA), and axons (output fibers). The brain houses billions and billions of neurons along with glial cells that nourish and support them, as well as contribute substantially to synaptic action. Of all the cells in the body, only neurons are capable of producing an electrochemical impulse; "firing" allows them to communicate with each other. After a neuron receives an adequate supply of chemicals from other neurons, an electrical impulse travels down the axon and "fires" its own neurotransmitters into the synaptic gap for other neurons to receive (see Figure 4.1).

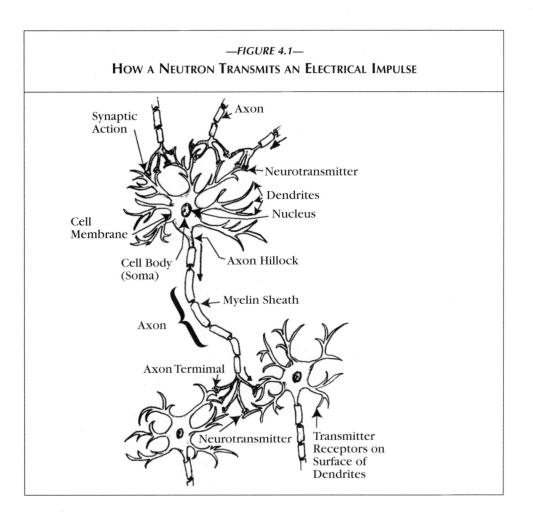

—*FIGURE 4.1*—
HOW A NEUTRON TRANSMITS AN ELECTRICAL IMPULSE

In *Organization of Behavior*, Donald Hebb (1949) suggests that learning occurs when neurons fire. Today, neuroscientists increasingly support Hebb's early inference that neuronal firing that is faster or slower than the base rate indicates information being processed (Guenther, 1998).

Since the time of Hebb's early work, scientists have learned that neurons that fire frequently remain active. This consistent active state is called *potentiation*, which causes neurons to increase their neurotransmitters and develop additional dendritic branches. Thus, both increase their ability to collect more information as learning occurs.

Some neurons' base firing rate is fast, however, while others naturally fire at a slower rate. Also, when stimulated by excitatory neurotransmitters, neurons increase their firing rate; when stimulated by inhibitory neurotransmitters, they fire slower than their base rate (Guenther, 1998). The more a neuron is stimulated by incoming signals, the faster or slower it fires depending on the type of chemical input. According to Guenther, "Currently, most neuroscientists believe that what is informative to the brain is whether a neuron is firing either faster or slower than its base rate" (p. 201).

Potentiation increases the potential for firing with less stimulation, and many researchers now believe long-term potentiation is probably *the* primary mechanism for learning to occur (Guenther, 1998). The more active the neuron, the greater its potential for contributing to a neuron network that creates awareness, perception, and learning—all aspects of consciousness. Consciousness of learning, however, also includes assigning an emotional or social valence to the experience: "Do I like what I am learning? Is this important to me?" Subjective analysis of an experience appears to be the essence of consciousness, and no one truly understands how the physiological functioning of neurons generates subjective experience.

Consciousness of learning, however, also includes assigning an emotional or social valence to the experience: "Do I like what I am learning? Is this important to me?" Subjective analysis of an experience appears to be the essence of consciousness, but no one truly understands how the physiological functioning of neurons generates subjective experience.

Purpose of Consciousness

The brain's complex systems orient us each morning when we awaken, allowing us to know where we are, who we are, and about what time it is. The brain stem again does its job automatically without our conscious effort. If it fails, our state of mind becomes disoriented and confused; we aren't certain if we are dreaming or awake. As we go about our business, the amygdala constantly produces emotional states and the brain stem spews out chemicals to orient us from one mind state to another. Still other neurons create images to help us make sense of how we feel. In this regard, "consciousness is the brain-mind's awareness of some of its own information" (Hobson, 1994, pp. 88 & 209).

By our own conscious self-talk and actions—such as getting adequate sleep, meditating, exercising, eating nutritious food, and monitoring our interactions with others—we can change our state of mind. Of course, adversity will come no matter how cheerful we are, but for the most part, we can make ourselves happy, sad, exhilarated, or miserable by consciously manipulating our thoughts, as discussed in Chapter 2. The better we are at turning devastating circumstances into positive learning experiences, the more others appreciate us as an inspirational example.

Without question, consciousness and how information is deciphered depend on brain structures, electrochemical neuronal activity, and interrelationships among numerous parallel systems and subsystems. From a psychological perspective, consciousness means being aware of feelings, thoughts, desires, actions, and reactions, and intentionally manipulating them. Without consciousness, we would respond to the internal and external worlds of our existence with automatic reflexes in much the same way our stomachs digest food without any direction from us. In other words, we would act like thoughtless jellyfish swimming through the sea of life.

Consciousness allows us to be *intentional*—to purposefully make plans, to thoughtfully consider pros and cons of a situation before taking action or leaving circumstances to sort themselves out, and to selectively and meaningfully determine courses of action toward our goals. Most adolescents are incredibly focused, intentionally self-directed, and extensively engaged in a sundry of meaningful activities. A small percentage, however, may simply be aware of going about a school routine with little thought toward influencing a possible outcome. Without deliberate and intentional action, youngsters tend to drift from one thing to another, failing to accomplish anything in particular. They exist in a state of selective helplessness, spending their time in some rather thoughtless way while the world goes by without them.

Early to mid-adolescence may be a time of tremendous waste of human potential, yet educators are often at a loss on how to engage academically withdrawn students. Perhaps we need to change *how* we teach students during this period of growth. Neurons dramatically increase during this time at a rate similar to that experienced during the first few months of life, and the potential for learning will never again be better. Jay Giedd, a researcher at the National Institutes of Health Child Psychiatry Branch, and his colleagues report that in a longitudinal Magnetic Resonance Imaging (MRI) study of 145 children ages 4 to 20 years, they found that "gray matter in the frontal lobe increased during pre-adolescence with a maximum size occurring at 12.1 years for males and 11.0 years for females" (Giedd et al., 1999, p. 861). This discovery was unexpected, because scientists had previously believed that no new neurons developed after about 18 months of age. The exciting news is that adolescent neuronal growth occurs at a time when students have control over what they choose to learn, and, therefore, which neurons live or die.

Consequently, teachers must provide meaningful stimulation that actively engages adolescents in making appropriate life choices. As part of this meaningful stimulation, we must guide adolescents to reach out and help others. Structured service programs through schools, clubs, or churches can provide the sense of competence, confidence, and contribution that builds adolescent character for a lifetime. Being engaged in meaningful experiences is critical throughout life, but especially during early adolescence.

Attention

No universally accepted definition for attention exists, but we know that it is a multidimensional concept involving cognitive and psychophysiological variables (Sergeant, 1996). Attention involves the following notions:

➤ Arousal (a physiological readiness to perceive stimuli)
➤ Consciousness
➤ Initial focus, sustained focus, and the capacity to shift focus
➤ The act of encoding (holding information briefly in memory long enough to perform an action or cognitive operation) (Halperin, 1996; Mirsky, 1996).

From a developmental perspective, an infant's attention appears to be driven by two forces: environmental stimuli and adults who intuitively direct a baby's attention ("Look here; see this ball. Look at Mommy."). Teachers continue directing children's attention with such comments as "Pay attention" and "Look at me." Infants also notice light and dark contrasts, things that move, and novelties. Quantity differences of three or four items draw their attention as well, and infants will lose interest if the number of items remains the same. When the quantity is changed, they will once again react vigorously (Diamond & Hopson, 1998).

Voluntary orientation develops by 4 years of age as children learn to scan their environment actively rather than responding to a novel stimulus. In other words, they actively select relevant stimuli and ignore irrelevant information (Halperin, 1996). By ages 5 or 6, children gain an internally driven attention mechanism; and as perceptual abilities mature for receiving input and motor abilities mature for output, children increase their capacity to sustain attention at will.

Sustaining attention long enough to process new information can be hard work, but sooner or later, information—at least some of it—becomes automatic if reviewed and practiced. We see evidence of this when reciting a favorite poem or learning to read. Reaching this level has its rewards. As individuals move from an effort-filled mode of processing—where we actively control attention—"to automatic processing that occurs without conscious awareness. . . , the amount of information that can be processed increases" (Halperin, 1996, p. 126).

Jeffrey Halperin, professor of psychology and neuropsychology at Queens College, City University of New York and expert on attention deficit hyperactivity disorder (ADHD), states that attention may switch across stimuli, allowing people to attend to various tasks, or focus on several stimuli simultaneously, making it "a mechanism of multiple channels of selectivity. If this were the case, as learning occurs and tasks become more automatic, not only could the capacity of any given channel increase, but so could the number of channels" (Halperin, p. 126). This means the more we learn via any intake channel—whether the channel be visual, auditory, tactual, social, or emotional—the greater our potential for learning many things at once.

Attention Deficit Disorder. Halperin (1996) maintains that orienting a child's attention—whether directed by the child or another person—is a necessary precursor for selective attention and further information processing. This is true even though selective attention may require children to ignore orienting responses to alternate and irrelevant stimuli (Halperin, 1996). Children with attention deficits have difficulty focusing their attention on anything unless it is new, includes novelty, and is highly stimulating or frightening (Amen, 1995). These features explain why children can stay "glued" to video games and action-packed television programs when they remain inattentive during calm classroom routines.

Another expert on ADHD, Russell Barkley (2000), director of psychiatry at the University of Massachusetts Medical Center, believes that the disorder is probably not a disturbance in selective or sustained attention, but rather a deficiency in inhibiting responses and the capacity to delay responding. That is, students would not know when *not* to react and *how* to wait. Apparently, the neurons fire in rather random ways without adequate inhibitory signals to put on the brakes.

What does this mean for teachers? First, children's attention is drawn to many interesting things and thoughts other than what the teacher is offering. To support the likelihood that children will attend to what teachers want, the academic task must be sufficiently interesting. The task also must remain varied enough to sustain students' attention. Second, once students attend to a lesson, they will make decisions about what they learn and construct their own meaning. Teachers need to ensure meaningful ways for students to use the information so it sticks with them. In addition, attention cannot be separated from memory, because selective and sustained attention depend on working and stored memory to give meaning to information (Sergeant, 1996).

Memory

The British physicist and biochemist Francis Crick (1994) describes memory as "internal representations"—or neuronally encoded and structured versions—of the external and internal milieu (an individual's world) that could potentially guide behavior. There is no single storage area for records of the past, but the physiology of learning and remembering reflects changes to neurons involved in perception, language, feeling, movement, and so on. Thus, memory is not a "thing," but a process of neuronal network activation (Hobson, 1994). According to the constructivist theory, the brain constantly "tunes" itself in response to experiences by changing the strength of connections among neurons. Even so, we now know that no neural tissue is dedicated exclusively to storing a record of specific experiences (Guenther, 1998).

Memory is distributed throughout the brain in various cognitive subsystems that perceive, reflect, and act on experiences. For example, damage to the occipital lobe can undermine visual perception and some types of implicit memory, whereas damage to the posterior and temporal lobes disrupts verbal memory (Greenfield, 1996). The hippocampus *seems* to modulate the formation of connections among neurons for recalling specific events in episodic memory (Greenfield). While speculative, this role appears to be reasonable because bilateral damage to the hippocampus causes amnesia for developing new memories. For example, while keeping memories of old events intact, you may not recall where you parked the car or whom you just met. Obviously, this condition can play havoc with developing relationships.

Together the hippocampus and amygdala generate emotional and other types of imagery, as well as attention, learning, and memory for long-term storage and retrieval of newly learned information. The amygdala also plays a role in activities related to reward, orientation, and attention, in addition to emotional arousal. If some event becomes associated with positive or negative emotional states, the amygdala is likely to remember it, as discussed in Chapter 2.

Memories are generally stored in either the right or the left hemisphere, but not in both. When the brain attempts to store memories in both, learning disabilities may result. Successful readers and math students, for example, unilaterally store language symbols in the left hemisphere, whereas those with reading and math disabilities tend to store language representations in both hemispheres. This mixed storage apparently creates confusion when recall is needed (Orbzut & Hynd, 1991).

The right hemisphere seems to store images as well as visual, emotional, musical, facial, and spatial information (including knowledge of the left half of the body). This suggests that split-brain research continues to be supported in part by recent findings. It is important to remember that memory and learning seem to lie in the reconfiguration of the synaptic connections—neural networks associated with the structures—rather than directly in the structure. Learning, therefore, seems to depend on the state of mind at the time learning opportunities are available and on which major learning system is in control. Because memories are stored as patterns of electrical sequences in the brain, remembering becomes a matter of activating particular electrical sequences out of the tens of billions residing in the brain in a resting or active state.

Functional View of Memory. There is an emerging consensus that the major memory systems of the mind include several different types of memory. First, the *functional view* divides memory into short-term and long-term memory. Whereas short-term was once thought to be separate from long-term memory, it is now considered to be "that portion of long-term memory that is temporarily at a heightened state of activation at a particular moment in time" (Wagner, 1996, p. 148). It functions as the locus of cognitive control for attention, because it determines where to direct peripheral attention, how to encode new inputs, and how to engage in the process of rehearsal.

According to Crick (1994), who collaborated with James Watson to discover the molecular structure of DNA, short-term memory can be subdivided by sensory type: visual, auditory, tactual, kinesthetic, and olfactory. Children who demonstrate a deficit in short-term auditory memory or short-term visual memory generally demonstrate serious reading difficulties that could result in identification of a learning disability, because children fail to retain the information long enough to store the new words heard or read in long-term memory. For Crick, *short-term* is in a range from 100 to 200 milliseconds to seconds and minutes. This amount of time allows for the processing of very brief signals and retention of about seven digits. By contrast, long-term memory can last for hours, days, months, or even years (Crick).

We can think of long-term memory in many ways. Many of the descriptions scientists use mean the same thing. For example, *explicit, declarative, categorical,* and *episodic* all refer to memory for facts, ideas, and events. By comparison, *implicit, nondeclarative, semantic,* and *procedural* refer to memory for skills, language, and actions. For purposes of simplicity, I use the terms *episodic* and *procedural* to discuss long-term memory.

Episodic memory describes memory for specific events or episodes in life with a specific time-space locus, such as remembering the death of a loved one; graduation ceremonies; the birth of a child; a family reunion; an automobile accident; where you were and what you were doing when President John F. Kennedy was assassinated, the Challenger exploded, the World Trade Center collapsed; or simply, where you parked your car or put your grade book. Generally, the more traumatic the episode, the greater the recalled detail is for the place, the weather, the colors and smells, people's voices, and other sounds of the event. Recall of events is sometimes called "one-shot" or "flashbulb" memory for obvious reasons. Verbalizing these kinds of memories over and over can strengthen them. The important features of episodic memory are its concrete nature, its sensory richness, and its conscious or active recall (Crick, 1994; Donald, 1991; Guenther, 1998).

Procedural memory differs from episodic memory because it involves learned action patterns. Whereas episodic memory preserves the specifics of events, procedural memory preserves the generalities of action across events, such as learning to drive a car and then driving it without constantly thinking about how the learning occurred (Donald, 1991). Procedural memories ignore specific episodic memories (e.g., making the winning basket in the regional basketball championships) but store the general patterns for creating the action (playing basketball). It would be burdensome to remember how each practice shot was made—the manner of dribble, your location for each shot, and all the other details—because the opportunity to make the basket may not match any of the specifics in practice. Procedural memory, then, involves setting parameters and forming general rules. Detailed episodic recall would interfere with this process (Donald).

Much of procedural memory relies on semantic or representational memory, which humans use to make them different from their ape cousins. "Where humans have abstract symbolic memory representations, apes are bound to the concrete situation or episode; and their social behavior reflects this situational limitation"

(Donald, 1991, p. 149). Semantic memory lets us retain an understanding of what words mean without remembering how we learned the word.

In *Human Cognition*, R. Kim Guenther (1998) describes a telling incidence of procedural or *implicit* memory from history. In the early 1970s, former Beatle George Harrison released a hit song entitled "My Sweet Lord." Unfortunately, the melody was nearly identical to "He's So Fine," released in 1962 by The Chiffons. When the lawsuit dust settled, Harrison paid for his mistake but insisted he had no recollection of hearing the song years earlier. He composed his melody without an accompanying conscious awareness that he had already learned it from a previously released song—an excellent example of procedural memory.

In summary, the functional view of long-term memory includes repeated opportunities to learn the language, skill, or action; lack of awareness of accessing memory to perform the act or use a word (procedural memory); and memory at a relatively automatic level (Guenther, 1998; Hobson, 1994; Joseph, 1996).

Constructivist View of Memory. Guenther (1998) argues that human memory is designed to anticipate the future rather than preserve the past. She maintains that each new experience changes neurons in one or more of the learning systems while adapting to repetitions of the same patterns of experience and their unexpected exceptions. No specific recorded account of the experience is stored anywhere in the brain, she concludes. Further, recall of the past involves a reconstruction process based on current information and future planning, rather than accessing stored records or reexperiencing the past. In other words, the person *actively* creates some plausible account of the past experience; forgetfulness is due to the continuous adaptive changes made in the various learning systems in response to events. Thus, constructionists view remembrance as a form of reconstruction in which various sources of knowledge are used to *infer* the past (Guenther). Cultural memories also play a significant role in the recall process. Guenther cites an experiment conducted by an Anglo-American psychologist, Frederic Charles Bartlett, as a good example of the constructive recall process. In *Remembering: A Study in Experimental and Social Psychology*, Bartlett presented his British subjects with an English translation of a Native American folk story called "The War of the Ghosts." He then asked them to recall details of the story after varying time intervals. As seen in Figure 4.2, recall was distorted and incomplete in terms of unfamiliar names, conceptual understanding of ghosts, and critical transitions. When subjects were ignorant of the Native American culture, they invented details in keeping with what they knew from their own culture.

—*FIGURE 4.2*—

THE TEXT OF "THE WAR OF THE GHOSTS" AND ONE SUBJECT'S RECOLLECTION OF IT

The War of the Ghosts

One night two young men from Egulac went down to the river to hunt seals, and while they were there it became foggy and calm. Then they heard war cries, and they thought: "Maybe this is a war party." They escaped to the shore, and hid behind a log. Now canoes came up, and they heard the noise of paddles, and saw one canoe coming up to them. There were five men in the canoe, and they said:

"What do you think? We wish to take you along. We are going up the river to make war on the people."

One of the young men said: "I have no arrows."

"Arrows are in the canoe," they said.

"I will not go along. I might be killed. My relatives do not know where I have gone. But you," he said, turning to the other, "may go with them."

So one of the young men went, but the other returned home. And the warriors went on up the river to a town on the other side of Kalama. The people came down to the water, and they began to fight, and many were killed. But presently the young man heard one of the warriors say:

"Quick, let us go home: that Indian has been hit." Now he thought: "Oh, they are ghosts." He did not feel sick, but they said he had been shot.

So the canoes went back to Egulac, and the young man went ashore to his house, and made a fire. And he told everybody and said:

"Behold I accompanied the ghosts, and we went to fight. Many of our fellows were killed, and many of those who attacked us were killed. They said I was hit, and I did not feel sick."

He told it all, and then he became quiet. When the sun rose he fell down. Something black came out of his mouth. His face became contorted. The people jumped up and cried.

He was dead.

Subject's Reproduction

Two youths were standing by a river about to start seal-catching, when a boat appeared with five men in it. They were all armed for war.

The youths were at first frightened, but they were asked by the men to come and help them fight some enemies on the other bank. One youth said he could not come, as his relations would be anxious about him; the other said he would go, and entered the boat.

In the evening he returned to his hut, and told his friends that he had been in a battle. A great many had been slain, and he had been wounded by an arrow, he had not felt any pain, he said. They told him that he must have been fighting in a battle of ghosts. Then he remembered that it had been queer and he became very excited.

In the morning, however, he became ill, and his friends gathered round; he fell down and his face became very pale. Then he writhed and shrieked and his friends were filled with terror. At last he became calm. Something hard and black came out of his mouth, and he lay contorted and dead.

Source: Reprinted with permission from Barlett, F. C. (1932). *Remembering: A study in experimental and social psychology.* Cambridge, England: Cambridge University Press. pp. 65, 72. Reprinted with permission of Cambridge University Press.

Later, Ulric Neisser supported Bartlett's work by announcing that remembering is like problem solving. We use existing knowledge and memories of previous reconstructions to create a plausible rendition of a particular past event (Neisser cited in Guenther, 1998). We may think we remember the past in accurate detail, but constructivist research has shown that the clearly remembered details could be highly inaccurate. To conclude her persuasive arguments for the constructivist view, Guenther states, "Because each new experience results in altering the strengths of connections among neurons, the brain is constantly 'tuning' itself in response to experiences. But it has no neural tissue dedicated only to storing a record of each experience" (p. 119).

Multiplex Cognitive Processing

As discussed in the previous two chapters, the emotional and social learning systems play a key role in how we cognitively process information. This is also true regarding factors within the cognitive system, including attention and memory.

According to A. R. Luria (1973), who studied the use of self-talk or thinking for the regulation of behavior, we regulate our actions by giving ourselves explicit directions. We also use self-talk to analyze situations and mediate between a previously constructed point of view and a conflicting incoming point of view. From this subtle but powerful analysis and mediation, we transform our thinking and belief systems. In the process, self-talk relies on various types of memory to attend to a stimulus for an extended period. Self-talk initially asks if the stimulus is new or something already experienced; the inquiry may consist of such conscious expressions as, "Something is different here. I better pay attention." Short-term memory allows for a quick analysis, followed by a rapid search of long-term and working memory. If self-talk analysis and mediation create a change in one's thinking and belief systems, memory is reconstructed to incorporate those changes.

How we consciously consider new input or contemplate past experiences relies heavily on interactions among the learning systems, including the physical and reflective systems (discussed in Chapters 5 and 6). At any one moment, all systems simultaneously vie for attention and control as if in a multiplex movie theater without walls. How does the cognitive system construct knowledge from competing or cooperative systems? To illustrate this complex and interrelated process, consider the following example of a World War II lesson.

As the teacher introduces the topic, students' individual learning systems are either activated or inhibited in response to each student's emotional-social-cognitive-physical-reflective mental state. Student reactions, therefore, will vary depending on their state of mind and the learning system most active at the time. For example, if the student is mentally concerned about a family crisis (emotional system) and World War II information is directed to the cognitive system, there may be little attention to the teacher's introduction. In this case, no new learning takes place because of inattention.

By contrast, let's say students pay attention and think about the teacher's lesson. They may focus their thoughts and consider how the new information is like something they already know, or they may ignore the information at this point. If the teacher's introduction seems like the same old thing, students may respond automatically, like experienced drivers stepping on the brake without consciously telling themselves to do so. In this case, their unconscious response prevents new learning. Another possibility is that students may briefly pay attention but may not think about the content, or they may attend long enough to consider only what is new, different, novel, or interesting. If they find nothing there to hold their attention, students begin thinking about something totally unrelated. Since their consciousness is focusing on something other than the lesson, they cognitively disengage and assume a neutral posture that clearly reveals a lack of interest and engagement.

Other students may find the new information exciting and meaningful. The idea of studying about World War II may remind them of a movie or a war story told to them by a favorite grandparent. They sharpen their focus and analyze the complexities, but suddenly they may feel jolted by new information that contradicts what Grandpa said. A mental conflict arises, and a decision point is automatically reached: Either believe what Grandpa said and keep what is already known without changing it (which would leave the existing understanding intact), or entertain the possibility that another point of view on the same situation is valid. If this latter decision is reached, the student may try to figure out how the two bits of information differ and contemplate why. This decision-making process requires sustained focus, searching for more information, and analysis in terms of details, ideas, and complexities; it also may require guidance from the teacher.

If the conflict is resolved, students assimilate new ways of thinking to produce newly constructed knowledge. At some point, the unit of study may require additional analysis to resolve more cognitive conflicts. In which case, the previously assimilated new information could be reanalyzed, synthesized, or elaborated to form newly reconstructed knowledge or to express the knowledge in creative ways. In contrast to this decision-making process, some students may respond marginally by finding out what the teacher wants them to learn and then attempting to memorize by repetition and rehearsal without any meaningful understanding. Students might drill themselves on the facts for rote recall and a good mark on an exam, but since neural systems are notoriously inept at retaining unrelated details, the memory is bound to be short-lived and the facts quickly forgotten.

The preceding example illustrates some of the complex factors and decision points students face as they weigh and consider new learning. Because each child is different, the individual's weighing and sorting are highly contingent on what learning system is most active at any one moment.

The nature of cognition is far more complex than depicted in this simple linear example. Cognition tends to be far more simultaneous than sequential and input can be processed in random ways, rather than in the step-by-step approach suggested by the previous scenario. Nonetheless, decision points arise as the mind weighs input and chooses to attend or not to attend. Neurons either fire or are inhibited as the mind compares new information with what is already "known" and as it struggles to construct and reconstruct meaning.

Educational Considerations

Listening, speaking, reading, writing, and other academic skill development depend on the cognitive system. The cognitive system depends on sensory input and the adequate functioning of the attention, information processing, and memory subsystems for the construction of knowledge and skills. Just as important, the cognitive system functions best when other systems—emotional, social, physical, or reflective—are not competing with it for attention. When systems compete rather than cooperate, learning is drastically diminished.

There is another critically important aspect to effective cognitive functioning in the classroom. Teachers must demonstrate enthusiasm and a keen grasp of the content they teach, because students quickly size up teachers and decide if they know and enjoy the material they expect children to learn. If it appears that teachers do not, children think, rightly or wrongly, "I know more about this than the teacher. Why should I listen to him?" When students feel the teacher's enthusiasm about the subject, that enthusiasm is contagious because it facilitates eagerness for learning and a desire for academic excellence. Teachers should be passionate about what they teach and demonstrate clear intentions and high expectations that children will also love the subject. Of course, teachers foster emulation when they exhibit acceptance and respect for students based on their strengths and learning-style preferences.

I began this book with the emotional and social learning systems because when they are in distress, they rob the cognitive system of the ability to focus attention on academics for problem solving and decision making. Thus, skill and knowledge acquisition take a distant second or third place in the mind's multiple operating systems. When systems compete, it is as if each system were playing a different movie in the separate but interrelated theaters of the mind (see Chapter 7). When this occurs, mental confusion reigns. Activation of multiple systems focused on the same "movie" will increase learning. When soliciting student engagement for difficult-to-learn tasks, teachers would be wise to make certain that tasks are personally relevant so the emotional learning system is focused. Also, as learning *facilitators*, teachers need to take the time to learn about each student's wishes, dreams, and desires and then use them to guide knowledge and skill development in keeping with positive goal attainment. This effort can go a long way toward promoting a positive code of classroom conduct. If the teacher fails to take the emotional and social learning systems into consideration, the theaters of the mind are apt to compete for attention, thus decreasing opportunities to learn.

When information that keeps coming into awareness is congruent with personal goals, thought flows effortlessly. As Csikszentmihalyi (1990) writes: "Attention can be freely invested to achieve a person's goals, because there is no disorder to straighten out, no threat for the self to defend against" (p. 40). Csikszentmihalyi calls the effortless state of sustained engagement the *flow experience*, and those who attain it develop a stronger, more confident self, because they successfully invest more of their energy in goals they choose to pursue (Figure 4.3).

Keeping the Cognitive Learning System in Balance

The cognitive learning system thrives on mental challenge and problem solving. This system's *need to know* states a genetic truth in simple terms: Humans are designed to learn. Learning is as natural as breathing, and it cannot be stopped short of brain damage. Even then, the need to know generally prevails. Because *knowledge* is so important to this system, traditional schooling has held cognitive learning in the highest esteem. National and state standards have singled it out as the meas-

---

—*FIGURE 4.3*—
How to Develop the "Flow Experience"

The Flow Experience

Mihaly Csikszentmihalyi said that as people describe how they feel when thoroughly enjoying themselves, eight distinct dimensions characterize the flow experience:

1. Clear goals: an objective is distinctly defined; immediate feedback: one knows instantly how well one is doing.

2. The opportunities for acting decisively are relatively high, and they are matched by one's perceived ability to act. In other words, personal skills are well suited to given challenges.

3. Action and awareness merge; one-pointedness of mind.

4. Concentration on the task at hand; irrelevant stimuli disappear from consciousness, worries and concerns are temporarily suspended.

5. A sense of potential control.

6. Loss of self-consciousness, transcendence of ego boundaries, a sense of growth and of being part of some greater entity.

7. Altered sense of time, which usually seems to pass faster.

8. Experience becomes autotelic: If several of the pervious conditions are present, what one does becomes autotelic, or worth doing for its own sake

Source: Csikszentmihalyi , M. (1993). *The evolving self: A psychology for the third millennium.*
New York: Harper Collins, p. 178-179. Reprinted with permission.

---

urement system for educational effectiveness at the near exclusion of other systems, even though it cannot function optimally without their full support. Children and adults who live exclusively in the cognitive system may isolate themselves from others and develop a head full of information without a clear way to use it.

However, young children who exercise their cognitive learning system ask meaningful questions that go beyond the usual "Why?" They ask how things work, what words mean, how to count objects, how fingernails grow, what color is the coldest, why thunder follows lightning, and what makes rain. They depend on adults to provide authentic answers that satisfy their need to know. Adult responses of "Because I said so," "You'll know when you're older," or "I don't know how it works; it just does!" send messages that curiosity and learning are unimportant. Conversely, teacher facilitators will respond with brief and accurate answers or help children find or create answers. These responses help stimulate new learning and additional inquiry.

The *intention* of the cognitive learning system is to develop new knowledge and skills. It also deliberately plans and prepares for transforming into realities *passions* generated by the emotional learning system and *visions* produced by cultural interactions. Without question, most children enter school eager to satisfy a strong need to know, but if they fail to keep up with their classmates, that need goes unsatisfied, and learning to read, write, and calculate may become horrific tasks to be avoided.

Teachers can stimulate and facilitate learning in all children by addressing the need to know in multiple ways. They must facilitate learning through lessons that optimize each of the natural learning systems. By providing alternative ways of learning through the different systems, students are at liberty to gain new information through those most comfortable for them. Giving students assignment options can enhance lessons generally taught by just reading and answering questions. For example, students can:

- act out the lesson's concepts
- create a poem
- write new lyrics to "Twinkle-Twinkle Little Star"
- recite a tap-tap-clap rap rhythm that includes the major points
- build the concepts with rods and explain how the construction conveys the ideas
- illustrate major points on a poster
- develop question and answer cards for an in-class quiz show
- construct a board game using the same cards as those used for the quiz game

There are countless ways to involve both active learners and students needing social interaction while addressing the lesson content and the needs of other students at the same time, without particular concern for the individual child's learning-style. Teachers can meet students' individual learning-style preferences generically while gaining a measure of comfort with systems instruction. Once this is accomplished, teachers can identify individual learning-style needs and help students use them for even greater control of their learning.

Identification of a learning disability is no excuse for academic failure. Only a small number of children are unable to learn within a satisfactory range when taught with alternative strategies based on learning-system strengths. Facilitating student learning through a systems approach, however, may require focused problem solving and new ways of teaching.

Although Csikszentmihalyi did not refer to congruence among the natural learning systems as necessary for focused attention, his description of the flow experience clearly suggests that deep and experiential learning occurs only when all systems are operating smoothly and alertly in Vygotsky's Zone of Proximal Development and attending to the same stimuli. Much of that experiential learning relies on the physical learning system, which keeps us actively engaged in the learning process.

5

The Physical Learning System

eople have always relied on the brain's physical system for food, shelter, clothing, social interactions, the building of communities, and leisure activities. The physical learning system executes what other brain systems contemplate, whether writing a novel, performing surgery, or constructing a skyscraper. Thus, some of the largest areas in the brain are devoted to hand activity and body movement. Over the years, however, educators have tended to treat the physical system as a necessary supporting system for learning or for sport, rather than as a learning system in its own right. Recent research has clearly shown that the body has exquisite influence on how the mind works (Conners, 1989; Hannaford, 1995; Rapp, 1996). In some ways, therefore, the body has a mind of its own, even though for decades, influential psychologists have attempted to convince us otherwise.

For example, both B. F. Skinner and Jean Piaget describe physical learning as the action of the physical environment on the child, rather than the actions of the child on the environment (Sprinthall, Sprinthall, & Oja, 1994). This is no doubt true when stepping on a tack or touching a hot iron. One learns quickly from environmental experiences that produce autonomic reflexes. Learning may also occur when a child's behavior prompts a positive or negative response from a caregiver or teacher; but because of the cyclical nature of such behavior and responses, it is difficult to determine who is creating the major influence. Is the child manipulating the adult, or is the adult manipulating the child?

My view is that the brain's physical learning system involves a process of interacting with the environment for the purpose of developing new knowledge and skills or expressing emotions or concepts. Using the physical learning system to learn new information, understand difficult concepts, and develop new skills is as important as demonstrating what you have learned through imitation or creative expression. Think of the variously talented people who draw, paint, dance, act, engage in sports, or play with ideas by building models or creating inventions. Brain systems for touch and movement are extensive, and teachers can use them to promote the learning of difficult concepts in a natural, biologically based way.

In the classroom, students with a strong need to be active generally find the use of *self-correcting manipulative materials* engaging as they develop knowledge and skills associated with the standards of learning. In fact, physically active students enjoy

> Constructing their own learning materials.
> Converting information to be learned into human-interest stories.
> Developing posters or other art products.
> Acting out historical or social events.

For physically active students, physical learning may involve food preparation to better understand a culture; game construction that captures information to be learned; and character identification whereby they share feelings and ideas as if they were characters found in literature, history, or social studies.

Because the brain's physical learning system depends extensively on tactile, tactual, and kinesthetic input, I first explore the dynamics of touch and then go on to movement. I then discuss the reactions of the brain's physical learning system to environmental stimuli, such as food and environmental toxins that influence thinking and behavior. I conclude the chapter with a brief exploration of the effect of the physical being on our learning process. As we shall see, the individual and environment act one on the other to produce meaningful insights.

Touch

Our common language is peppered with terms associated with touch: Diane Ackerman (1990), staff writer for *The New Yorker* and recipient of the Academy of American Poets' Peter I.B. Lavan Award, wrote an insightful book called *A Natural History of the Senses.* In this poetic approach to sensory input, Ackerman speaks about how some things *touch* us deeply; solving problems can be *smooth, thorny, ticklish, sticky,* or *handled with kid gloves* (Ackerman, 1990). It is difficult to communicate with *touchy* people, she writes, while *touchy-feely* people engulf us with endless praise. *Out of touch* translates to uninformed while *losing touch* suggests loss of one's mental faculties. *Toccata* in music is intended to show touch technique while *touché* means to be touched with a fencing foil or by someone's well-made augmentative point (Ackerman; Damasio, 1999).

We often use two words interchangeably when speaking about the sense of touch: *tactile* and *tactual*. Strictly speaking, the first refers to the sense of *being touched*: feeling the wind blow against the skin, experiencing someone's hand on your shoulder, and so forth. Tactual is the act of touching and manipulating, generally with the hands.

The distinction between tactile and tactual may be more clinical than applied because both often co-occur; that is, simultaneous touching and being touched. To illustrate: Allen, a 9-year-old student diagnosed as emotionally troubled/learning disabled, excitedly tore newspaper strips and awaited a dish of wheat paste so he could cover a wire-framed giraffe he had carefully constructed. As soon as he immersed the first strip, he started jumping, screaming, and waving his paste-covered hand frantically: "Get it off me! Get it off me!" The feel of the cool, goolike substance frightened and confused him, but when provided a bottle of glue, he happily pasted one strip of paper at a time and completed a papier-mâché giraffe any 9-year-old would be proud to claim. Humans and primates need touch—both tactile and tactual touch. Yet, like Allen, some people prefer touching certain substances whereas other substances may be intolerable.

Tactile Touch

"It's amazing how much information is communicable in a touch. Every other sense has an organ you can focus on, but touch is everywhere" (Tiffany Field, cited in Ackerman, 1990, p. 74). Being touched can convey safety and signal the body to develop, or it can convey pain. Further, touch-starved people of all ages sicken and emotionally wither. Ackerman writes about how Saul Schanberg, a Duke University experimental neurologist, investigates pediatric disorders by working with rats. Schanberg says touch is "ten times stronger than verbal or emotional contact, and it affects damn near everything we do. No other sense can arouse you like touch;" he continued, "we always knew that, but we never realized it had a biological basis" (p. 77). He found that when licked and groomed by their mothers, rat pups produced growth hormones, but when the pups were removed from mother's care, their production of growth hormones dropped. On mother's return or when provided simulated grooming with a paintbrush, the pups overreacted and required significantly more touching to regain normal response patterns. "Touch," says Ackerman, "reassures an infant that it's safe: it seems to give the body a go-ahead to develop normally" (p. 77).

This finding is not surprising, because at least six kinds of microscopic sensors lie in the dermis—the layer of skin immediately beneath the dead outer layer of epidermis—and each type of sensor responds to various types of sensations: warmth, touch, pain, cold, itch, tickle, vibration, pressure, temperature, movement; and different types of pain, such as burning/searing, throbbing/aching, stabbing, and sharp (Ackerman, 1990). The skin is the largest organ of the human body, and all varieties of touch involve the skin. At the same time, the skin's sensors stimulate emotional reactions that are as important as their practical functions.

Researchers now know that specific types of tactile stimulation of the skin send messages to the brain that stimulate the production of oxytocin and endorphins. As discussed earlier, oxytocin promotes bonding between mother and infant, and endorphins—opiate-related peptides—produce a sense of well-being (Sylwester, 1995). It is well documented that babies in foundling homes die in infancy or grow up with severe difficulties relating to others if not handled and stroked—presumably because essential chemicals produced by being touched fail to get activated during critical periods.

Children whose needs for positive touch are not met at home or at school produce stress hormones, such as cortisol, that not only tighten muscles, but also reduce the brain's ability to concentrate and learn (Hannaford, 1995). Being touched is important for adults and the elderly, as well. Ackerman (1990) reports on a Purdue University experiment whereby a librarian brushed the hand of half the students as they checked out books. On leaving the library, the investigators asked the students several questions about their satisfaction with the library services. Those whose hands were touched reported significantly higher levels of satisfaction—and life in general—than those not touched. They rated the librarian friendlier, but they were unaware they had been touched. As subtle as this small gesture was, it clearly demonstrated the effect of touch on adults.

In today's society, where fear of inappropriate touch of children by adults is high, school personnel—especially those working with adolescents—may deliberately refrain from touching a student's hand, shoulder, or arm out of concern that the touch may be misinterpreted. Further, if students have a history of physical or sexual abuse, or if they suffered from touch deprivation during the early years, they may be exceedingly fearful of any type of teacher touch. Children and adults who suffer from lack of tactile stimulation are stripped of opportunities to produce brain chemicals—endorphins—that bond individuals and produce a sense of well-being in the classroom. Consequently, families must provide touch stimulation not only for preschoolers and elementary students, but for adolescents and each other, as well. Unless they do, the brain's predisposition for being touched will go unsatisfied. The subsequent production of harmful stress chemicals can result in limited learning and even brain damage (Restak, 1993/1994).

Figure 5.1 describes some ways that healthful touch exercises can be integrated into the curriculum. Touch releases tension and relieves stress. As several animal experiments demonstrate, touch is just as critical for primates as it is for humans.

Research on Monkey Touch

In a fascinating series of experiments conducted at the University of Wisconsin, researchers separated mother monkeys from their infants by a glass screen, others by a glass screen with holes large enough for them to touch one another, and others were separated in isolated environments. No serious problems developed for monkeys who could touch their mothers through holes in the glass, but monkeys reared in isolation and those who could see, smell, and hear their mothers but could not touch them suffered damage to the cerebellum (Ackerman, 1990).

Perhaps you recall Harlow's monkey experiments of the early 1960s. The profoundly important research went something like this: When given a terry-cloth surrogate "mother" that provided milk versus a wire-frame mother that also provided milk, babies with the warm, cloth "mother" close to their skin grew up able to explore new environments and situations in a masterful way whereas babies of wire-frame "mothers" exhibited bizarre adult behavior similar to schizophrenia. Further, babies of wire-frame "mothers" failed to relate to unfamiliar objects, and they were unable to mate (Sapolsky, 1994).

Daniel Alkon (1992), former chief of the Neural Systems Laboratory at the National Institutes of Health, said that genetics predesigns the monkey's brain to prefer certain patterns of sensory stimulation just as genetics predesigns human brains to seek emotional warmth and stimulation. In either case, the environment satisfies or fails to satisfy the human or monkey's established emotional needs for

---

—FIGURE 5.1—
WAYS TO ADD TOUCH EXERCISES TO THE CURRICULUM

The Art of Group Touch and Self-Touch

Touch exercises can safely be added to the curriculum to relieve tension and stimulate the release of emotional chemicals. Hannaford suggested an exercise whereby a child lies face down on the floor and pretends to be a car going through a car wash or a pizza being made. With their hands making different swishing, scrubbing, and sprinkling motions, several classmates "wash the car" and then blow on the car-child to dry it before another child takes a turn. In a workshop with adults, the exercise felt quite safe and nurturing. It may be worthy of exploration with children.

Teachers could lead children in self-touch such as the following:
1. Put your fingers of both hands on the back of your neck and apply pressure. Move your fingers up and down the upper spinal cord and brain stem especially where the skull and spinal cord meet.
2. Move the hands down and massage the muscles along the collarbone (clavicle).
3. Apply pressure on especially tender areas for a few seconds and quickly release them. Pressure points store tension which can dissipate with this simple technique.
4. Beginning at the top, unroll your ears and gently tug at the lobes, and massage along the inside curves of the outer ear where many acupuncture points are located.
5. Massage behind the ears and along the sides of the neck.
6. Wrap your arms around yourself tightly but comfortably until your fingers almost meet in back. Massage those areas under your fingertips along the shoulder blade (scapula).
7. Fold your arms, and stroke and massage the biceps.
8. Rub your hands together like two sandpaper blocks to build heat, then hold your hands an inch or two apart and feel the magnetic pulsating dance between the hands.
9. Wring your hands as if by washing them without soap or water. Interweave the fingers and move the hands back and forth to massage the fingers.
10. One at a time, twist and pull on your fingers as if taffy were difficult to get off.
11. Place the middle finger of each hand on the forehead above the eyebrow and apply slight pressure. Hold it for 30–60 seconds and release.
12. Place the middle finger on the temples and the thumbs in front of the ear lobe on the temporal-mandibular joint. Apply slight pressure at the temples and massage the joints with the thumbs. About 20 percent of all messages to and from the brain are affected by the temporal-mandibular joint, which tightens under stress, gets damaged with tooth grinding at night, and can cause severe headaches and mimic other illnesses.

You get the idea. These techniques not only feel good, they relieve tension by relaxing the muscles. Also, self-touch can send positive signals to the brain, and thereby produce chemicals conducive to enhanced self-esteem, higher levels of concentration, and increased academic achievement. Further, they can help condition fearful youngsters to accept appropriate touch from others—an essential behavior for healthy adulthood.

Source: Reprinted with permission from: Given, B. K. (1997). Emotional learning: Getting back to the basics. *Wisconsin School News, 52*(5), pp. 8-18.

nurturance and protection. During critical periods, the research monkeys who were deprived of stimulation learned that their needs were consistently unsatisfied by the surrogate mother, and, as a result, developmental and learning-induced changes occurred in their neural networks. Thereafter, their brains expected consistent deprivation, and this expectation helped determine all their future interests and experiences. Deprivation interfered with normal social relationships by producing expectations for solitude and unsuccessful interactions with others.

Researchers found that after periods of separation from their mothers, baby monkeys appeared helpless, confused, and depressed. Emotionally, they tended to regain normal behavior after constant holding for a few days, but their disturbed heart rates, body temperature, brain-wave patterns, sleep patterns, and immune system functions failed to return to normal after reuniting with their mothers.

Deficient environments not only prevent the availability of what the brain needs for normal growth, but also create brain abnormalities. The brain is prepared to select what it needs from the environment, and it uses its propensity for getting what it needs from whatever the environment provides. Consequently, a deprived baby, infant, and toddler may cry, scream, withdraw, or in some other ways behave "badly" to secure the attention of an adult who will touch it—even if that touch is harsh and abusive. Unfortunately, as implied earlier, abnormal neural connections become "hard-wired" the more they are reinforced, and reinforcement can lead to abnormal and ineffective brain development and behavior that last a life time (Alkon, 1992; Gazzaniga, 1992). Thus, maladaptive or deviant behavior may serve to get attention, but such behavior sets into motion the existence of neural networks that become "programmed" to obtain touch and social interactions of a negative type. Both Harlow and Alkon contend that neural networks first established become the most used networks when the organism is in crisis or under stress; therefore, the type of touch received during critical periods sets the stage for a person's lifelong experiences.

Fortunately, the brain has properties of plasticity that allow alterations of neural connections throughout childhood. Critical periods immediately after birth to age 3 appear to be of greatest importance in the establishment of healthy neural networks, followed by periods of neural development that serve children from age 3 to adulthood. Along the way, the brain can modify unhealthy networks; but the older the child, the more difficult modifications are for the human brain. In fact, many educators have designed early childhood education programs for children in low socioeconomic communities to combat the negative effects of deprivation and adverse home environments. The emphasis on "early childhood" is important because with age, neural flexibility diminishes until networks are fairly well established by age 15 or 16. Also, even with plasticity and behavioral change, specific brain structures hold memories of previous ways of responding. When the person is under stress or in a crisis, previous behavior may once again surface—as the brain's initial learned way of dealing with adversity. Thus, initial tactile learning maintains a strength beyond remolding with new learning, and it sets into motion positive or negative types of behavior that affect the learning of all the brain's systems (Alkon, 1992; Goleman, 1995; LeDoux, 1996). Therein lies the importance of tactile input; it cannot be overstated.

Tactual Learning

In addition to tactile input, early learning begins with movement and tactual input, and it develops sequentially to build a foundation for later academic learning. Most children move from gross-motor exploration for learning about the environment to fine-motor manipulation of objects, then to visual and auditory learning as the primary means of taking in information. Many students, however, retain a need for manipulating materials with their hands or large muscles when acquiring new skills. People with missing or malformed upper limbs due to birth defects or amputation may use their toes to manage paintbrushes, pencils, clothing, and objects. In either case, reaching out for exploration and learning by touching is *tactual;* and it comprises a large portion of the brain, including much of the "motor strip," as well as complex neural networks that connect the eyes, hands, and cerebellum. By contrast, some children lack eye-hand coordination and find the use of small muscles for holding a pencil and writing difficult. Historically, children lacking in manual dexterity have been incorrectly viewed as limited intellectually, because when the eyes and hands lack coordination, building with blocks, buttoning clothing, holding eating utensils, tying shoelaces, zipping jackets, and cutting with scissors are laborious tasks. For all children—clumsy or well-coordinated—touching objects and manipulating them serves as the cornerstone for later mental development, such as understanding direction (above, under, over, through, around), depth, shape, texture, weight, and volume.

Because more children prefer learning new information by handling it rather than by other sensory input (Dunn & Dunn, 1992, 1993), the time it takes teachers to translate information into hands-on and kinesthetic learning is well worth the effort for all concerned. So long as tactual learners can handle the information to be learned, they are more successful at learning it.

Kinesthetic Learning

Even though civilization has evolved from hunting and gathering to reading, writing, and computing, humanity continues to rely on the brain's physical learning system for survival and leisure activities. Kinesthetic learning begins to present itself while still in the womb, as baby kicks, squirms, and sucks its thumb; and kinesthetic learning continues after birth as flailing legs and arms gradually come under the control of purposeful actions.

Some children demonstrate early, persistent awkwardness in gross-motor skills when they move their arms, legs, torso, hands, and feet. They appear clumsy when playing with other children their age; and they have difficulty learning to skip, jump rope, throw or catch a ball, or sometimes peddling a tricycle or riding a scooter. Some children have no difficulties with gross-motor activities associated with kinesthetic learning, but they demonstrate difficulties with the manual dexterity necessary for writing and fine-motor movement. Being strong or weak in one area does not predict the same in the other, because different brain areas are involved.

Kinesthetic learning involves the whole body, its balance, and its position in space. In her popular book, *Smart Moves: Why Learning Is Not All in Your Head*, neurophysiologist and educator Carla Hannaford (1995) explains how vital the vestibular system is to movement and the integration of sensory input. She said that the vestibular system in the ear structure is fully developed by five months after conception, and that it is the first myelinated system—that is, neural axons are surrounded by insulating fat cells called *myelin* that make them function effectively. The vestibular system is considered the most sensitive of all sense organs because cilia (hair cells) respond to the motion of fluid to keep the head upright.

The vestibular system is composed of two components within the inner ear: the vestibular sacs and the semicircular canals. The vestibular sacs (the saccule and uticle) respond to gravity and keep the brain informed about the orientation of the head—whether it is up, down, to the side, or swung to the back. The semicircular canals respond to changes in the rotation of the head during movement, such as walking, running, and horseback riding (Carlson, 1995; Hannaford, 1995). Messages travel from the vestibular system to the brain stem's reticular activating system (RAS).

The RAS, in turn, responds with a wake-up call to the brain and gets us ready to learn (Carlson, 1995; Hannaford, 1995). Messages also travel to the cerebellum, spinal cord, medulla, pons, and temporal cortex to prompt movement.

Associated with the vestibular system, the propreoceptive system gives the sense of the body's position in space by sending messages to the motor cortex of the brain so it can execute balanced movements. Hannaford (1995) stresses that without movement, we cannot take in information from the environment because connections between the vestibular system and the neocortex, eyes, and muscles need movement to operate. We become awkward and clumsy in gait. Further, our eye movements tend to become jerky when experiencing stress, because stress alerts us for fighting or fleeing and interferes with balance. Touch and propreoception allow us to reach out and experience the environment. They help us organize our visual knowledge of dimension, texture, shape, size, line, and order and orient us to our surroundings (Hannaford).

It is easy to see that the vestibular system is critical to learning. In fact, when children are taught specific exercises to improve balance and movement, their learning improves (Hannaford, 1995, Chapter 13). Hannaford reported that the simple exercise of drawing large, "Lazy 8s" (the infinity sign) with outstretched arms and watching the hands cross the midline of the body can make a dramatic difference in reading fluency. This activity is designed to get the left and right brain hemispheres working in unison. It also allows the eyes to become aligned by reducing their outward focus created by stress when alert for danger. This exercise "centers" people temporarily and allows energy to flow throughout the nervous system.

To demonstrate the power of Lazy 8s, I often ask graduate students to read for one minute, count the number of words read, then make large Lazy 8s on the chalkboard while reciting one letter of the alphabet with each intersection. They then read for another minute and count the number of words read. Generally, they read at least 20 percent more words the second time and are amazed at their own fluency. For more information on specific proprioceptive activities, consult your local *Brain Gym* organization (Educational Kinesiology) (see Dennison & Dennison, 1994) and refer to Hannaford's (1995) *Smart Moves.*

Eating Your Way to Learning

From a neurobiological perspective, one could say that learning begins in the stomach, because fundamental building blocks of the brain and body begin with nutrition (Given, 1998). Because the immune system, the endocrine system, and the brain contain some of the same types of chemicals and chemical receptors (Pert, 1997), what we put in our stomachs affects how we think and how we act (Conners, 1989; Pert, 1997; Rapp, 1996; Wurtman & Suffes, 1996/1997). Proteins and carbohydrates consumed in our foods go through lengthy processes that eventually convert them to brain and body chemicals. Some foods create high energy, whereas other foods produce a calm demeanor, and still others produce physical stress.

Proteins

For example, enzymes in the stomach act on meats, beans, seeds, nuts, grains, and other protein foods to trigger the release of different amino acids, including the important tyrosine (Wurtman & Suffes, 1996/1997). Once in the bloodstream, tyrosine travels to the brain and becomes L-dopa; L-dopa loses atoms and triggers the release of dopamine that shoots from thousands of midbrain cell endings to produce a general feeling of alertness, attentiveness, quick thinking, rapid reactions, motivation, and mental energy (Pert, 1997). Tyrosine also triggers catecholamine amino acids that help produce alertness (Howard, 1994).

People often self-administer dopamine precursors by consuming caffeine drinks, chocolate, alcohol, marijuana, or other feel-good endorphins that may range from fairly harmless to seriously addictive (Restak, 1993/1994). When people do not get enough tyrosine in their systems from the foods they eat and they resort to self-administered variations, the less healthful variations often become habit forming and reduce the desire for protein intake from foods. Mild to severe malnutrition can occur from poor diets even in families with ample resources to provide nutritious foods. Of major importance, insufficient protein intake can cause fluids from inside the cells to seep out, causing sluggishness, limited concentration, stomach bloating, and the loss of essential salts and nutrients (Spreen, Risser, & Edgett, 1995).

Overall diet and especially protein intake may be even more critical than previously envisioned. Since the discovery that the human genome includes far fewer genes than previously considered to distinguish us from worms, scientific inquiry has shifted toward proteins as the true working parts of human mental machinery (Hawkes, 2001). Scientists hypothesize that there are no major qualitative differences between our brains and those of animals in terms of proteins, but there is a difference of size and complexity of the cross-links of the 250,000 proteins manufactured by the 30,000 or so genes. Uncurling the chains of amino acids that produce proteins will be far more complex than deciphering the genetic code, because these strings curl and fold in individually unique ways for health or illness (Hawkes). Thus, the direct relationship of diet on protein production and mental functioning is less clear than it was once thought to be, but it remains clear that children require sufficient intake of protein to function effectively, mentally, and physically.

For example, children who suffer from fear of failure, psychological isolation, and various forms of chronic stress need high levels of protein intake, but they are apt to be the children who receive only minuscule amounts in their diets. If so, their systems convert the limited amount of dopamine-produced alertness chemical into norephinephrine-controlled agitation and aggression in a matter of seconds. Without adequate protein, children may vacillate from aggression to apathy, nonresponsiveness, inactivity, and mild forms of irritability. Conversely, when children and adults eat more protein than is needed for brain functioning, it is stored in the muscles for ready access (Wurtman, 1988).

Complex Carbohydrates

In comparison to proteins, complex carbohydrates from foods such as pastas, vegetables, and breads convert into glucose (sugars) that enter the bloodstream and trigger the production of insulin and an amino acid called tryptophan (Wurtman & Suffes, 1996/1997). Insulin powerfully pushes glucose and amino acids into muscles for energy when needed. Tryptophan is then free from competition with other amino acids to travel to the brain where it is synthesized into serotonin. As discussed in Chapter 2, serotonin is a stress-reducing neurotransmitter that increases a positive sense of self and leadership. Limited intake of complex carbohydrates, by contrast, increases depression, low self-esteem, and a desire for sweets or simple sugars (Wurtman & Suffes). Unfortunately, simple sugars can be devastating to learning, because they create a rapid increase in insulin and a "sugar high" that is quickly followed by an overwhelming sense of sleepiness and foggy thinking. Of course, a large intake of complex carbohydrates can also cause a "sugar high," but it tends to reach a crescendo more slowly and last longer before gradually fading. A poor diet—limited intake of nutritious foods and high intake of simple sugars—stimulates aggressive behaviors when low blood sugar levels create mild forms of hypoglycemia. In a study reported by C. Keith Conners (1989) of Children's Hospital, Washington, D.C., 9- to 11-year-old children became impulsive and attended to irrelevant stimuli when their blood sugar levels fell after skipping breakfast. Children with chronically low blood sugar demonstrated poor reading and poor general achievement.

Refined Sugar

In 91 normal 4- and 5-year-old children Conners investigated, 40 percent of their daily diet was in the form of refined sugar—almost twice as much as adult consumption. Further, these children maintained high sugar consumption over the several months of the study, indicating a stable pattern of sugar intake beginning early in life. Those in the highest 25 percent of sugar consumers were significantly poorer on measures of attention, compared to those in the lowest 25 percent. Even more startling, the more sugar children ate (and the less protein), the higher were their observed aggressions (Conners, 1989). In fact, both children and adults became aggressive, violent, and seriously emotionally disturbed when they suffered low blood sugar crashes from a pattern of high sugar intake (Stitt, 1997).

If their blood sugar levels were low, even normally functioning men approved of violent acts and outwardly directed aggression when asked to rate violent acts on a paper-and-pencil questionnaire (Conners, 1989; Stitt, 1997). Reportedly, on an annual basis, the average American consumes 147 pounds of sugar and drinks 22 gallons of carbonated beverages that contain high amounts of sugar or artificial sweeteners—which are even more harmful than sugar (Rapp, 1996).

Anxieties and aggression produced by low blood sugar may be dramatically reduced during class sessions by permitting students to nibble on complex carbohydrates that raise the serotonin level. Furthermore, because many students from across socioeconomic groups suffer from poor eating habits, they may also need high protein intake to stimulate a relaxed alertness produced when tyrosine triggers the production of dopamine. In this case, peanut butter or trail mix with a high percentage of nuts and seeds may do the trick, provided students are not allergic to them. If the brain does not crave carbohydrate or protein intake while studying, students leave it alone once the novelty of having food in the classroom wears off. Roland Andrews (1990) and Pete Stone (1992), elementary school principals, reported less classroom mess when food was permitted than without it, because students learned to guard the privilege by monitoring spillage.

Unfortunately, teachers and parents often fail to recognize the direct relationship between sugary foods and their negative side effects. Rather, they attempt to treat the consequences while ignoring the causes. A vicious cycle ensues as diet-produced negative behavior and subsequent disciplinary actions increase while academic achievement and a sense of positive self-esteem decrease. Continued repetitions of disruptive behaviors, including anger and aggression, can easily become reinforced.

Aspartame

Part of the problem of aggressive behavior may stem from contaminants in the foods children consume. For example, the use of artificial sweeteners such as aspartame—a compound used in diet drinks, various brands of chewing gum, mints, and numerous food products including Kool Aid and Swiss Miss—is known to create serious behavior problems in children and adults (Conners, 1989; Rapp, 1996). Conners reported on a child who consumed Kool Aid sweetened with aspartame (NutraSweet) on specific days and Kool Aid sweetened with sugar on other days with the times of consumption being one week apart. In this "double-blind" study, neither the parents nor the clinicians knew on which days the child consumed the aspartame- versus the sugar-sweetened drink. When the child received aspartame, however, he demonstrated 70 percent more aggressive, angry, and defiant behavior followed by signs of exhaustion, withdrawal, irritability, headaches, and blurred vision than when he consumed the sugar-sweetened drink. Also, his appetite, sleep, and bladder control were disturbed.

Aspartame consists of two amino acids (aspartic acid, 40 percent, and phenylalanine, 50 percent) that naturally occur in the brain. It also contains methanol (10 percent). Phenylalanine is consumed in food products—especially protein—and is an essential precursor for the synthesis of dopamine and norepinephrine that tend to produce relaxed alertness. Heavy concentrations of phenylalanine, as found in artificial sweeteners, however, seem to disrupt the balance in the dopamine-norepinephrine system, especially in young children who are in the process of developing this system. Phenylalanine tends to lower levels of tyrosine needed for alertness; and this, in turn, upsets the production of norepinehrine, thus upsetting the "fight-flight" reaction, emotionality, and mood (Conners, 1989).

Enzyme action breaks phenylalanine down to avoid a buildup, and when that enzyme is missing in utero, a baby is born with phenylketonuria (PKU)—a condition leading to mental retardation if not properly treated. Even with the enzyme, phenylalanine can build up in the brain when concentrations are introduced in the form of artificial sweeteners. Headaches, blurred vision, and even seizures have been attributed to diet sodas and other products containing aspartame.

Methanol (methyl or wood alcohol), the third ingredient in aspartame, is a foreign, toxic substance to the brain that breaks down into formaldehyde (embalming fluid) and then formic acid—another name for ant poison. Methanol attacks the optic nerve and can cause vertigo, blurred vision, and even blindness at low doses and death in large doses (McMurry, 1984).

Aspartame is only one of hundreds of products now on the market or found in the home that can change children's behaviors abruptly or within 15 minutes to one hour after ingesting it (Rapp, 1996). Further, environmental toxins, such as disinfectants, room sprays, lead and chlorine in drinking water, radiation emitted from fluorescent lights, chemicals in carpets, pesticides in foods, growth hormones in milk, and formaldehyde as found in some toothpastes and facial tissues, as well as numerous other sources, may prompt hyperactivity and aggressive behavior in children allergic to these substances (Rapp, 1996). Teachers who see negative changes in a child's mood, temperament, and ability to write and learn should keep a record of what the child consumed at school and what sprays or air pollutants were used in the school environment. Then parents should be informed of these findings so they may have their child evaluated for allergies. Above all, teachers must refrain from giving simple sugars (candy) and artificially sweetened substances to children.

Mind-Body Connection

Pert (1997) underscored the relationship between the physical body and the mind by stating that the body becomes the battlefield for war games of the mind. Evidence that nerve fibers physically link the nervous system with the immune system makes Pert's battlefield analogy a powerful one (Felten, 1993). David Felten, professor of neurobiology and anatomy at the University of Rochester School of Medicine, notes: "Now there is overwhelming evidence that hormones and neurotransmitters can influence the activities of the immune system, and that products of the immune system can influence the brain" (p. 215). For example, two messages from the brain contribute to diminished immune system responses: lack of control of the situation and loneliness—a point discussed earlier in terms of children feeling isolated in school.

In Chinese medicine, human emotions—joy, anger, melancholy, brooding, sorrow, fear, and shock—are closely related to health and disease. Similarly, Robert Sapolsky (1994), author of *Why Zebras Don't Get Ulcers*, found that stress hormones from the adrenal gland can kill short-term memory cells in the brain. Also, decreased blood flow to the brain from "hardening of the arteries" affects the same brain cells as do stress hormones (Felten, 1993), whereas physical exercise with thoughtful concentration to identify where energy starts and how it moves through the body can keep the body and mind healthy (Eisenberg, 1993b). David Eisenberg, a member of the teaching staff of Dongzhimen Hospital in Beijing, where Western and Chinese medicine exist side by side, states:

> In Chinese medicine there's the idea that the body has to move, and that movement is as important as eating or sleeping or drinking. . . . If you don't move the body every day, it . . . is like a hinge on a door: if it is not swung open, it rusts. . . . The body has to reflect the balances in nature. So, as the seasons change, people are supposed to be outside in the seasons, and when they're outside, they're supposed to feel their energy. When they feel their energy, they can become balanced, but if they don't feel their energy, then they fall out of balance, and they get sick. . . . To maintain health, you have to have physical movement; . . . you have to control not only your physical body, but also your will and intention and your thoughts. Without that mental overlay, the physical movements are just superficial calisthenics. (pp. 277–281)

Relationships between the mind and body are just beginning to be understood in terms of health and learning. The study of ancient Chinese folk wisdom of 24 centuries ago when people lived to be 100 may shed some light on this relationship, as Western and Eastern researchers are beginning to grasp the neurological mind-body properties associated with physical learning reflected in Chinese medicine. As Eisenberg (1993a) states:

> I am more and more convinced that to understand health, I can't limit my study just to the physical body. I also have to understand the mind and spirit. (p. 314)

Educational Considerations

What can educators do with research about the physical learning system? Can we touch children in loving, caring ways without violating the "hands-off-students" policy designed to protect children? I believe we can. By saying to students, "That was a superb job! May I shake your hand? (. . .pat you on the back? . . .give you a hug? . . . give you a high five?)" we are conveying warmth while also giving children the authority to respond within their comfort zones. If a slight touch unnoticed by college students changed how the library services and the librarian were perceived, then incidentally touching a child's hand could trigger brain chemicals that help a child feel worthwhile in the classroom—provided the touch is coming from a nurturing person.

With regard to tactual and kinesthetic input, teachers can transform any concept or idea—no matter how abstract—into manipulative materials or experiential activities, such as play acting, authentic problem-solving, active games, art projects, or service learning. The list is limited only by a teacher's lack of imagination and unwillingness to explore and experiment with active alternatives to traditional paper-and-pencil tasks. If educators believe in the old mission statement, "Take each child where he or she is and teach from there," then we must accept the fact that the majority of children need physical activity and hands-on experiences to develop academic skills. No rational teacher expects children to change how they learn any more than they expect children to change their eye color. Yet, when children are required to spend at least five hours a day in environments unfriendly to how they learn, is it any wonder many children lose interest in the schooling process?

Keeping the Physical Learning System in Balance

The brain's physical learning system transforms passions, visions, and intentions into *actions* because this operating system is propelled by the *need to do*. Obviously, the physical system likes movement, activity, and hands-on learning; and the neurobiological structures and networks busily accommodate.

Math and science teachers have long known the value of manipulatives for helping students learn abstract concepts: Math teachers use Cuisenaire rods to teach mathematical comparisons, and science teachers use colored sticks and Styrofoam balls to build models of molecules. Manipulatives have their place in language arts, too. They can help students "see" the main idea and structure of a reading, as well as identify opportunities for revision of their writing.

Relationships between manipulatives and the physical learning system may appear obvious: Students use fine-motor skills and eye-hand coordination to build models. Students often choose to stand up at their work area as they build to see their models from a bird's-eye view. They constantly touch and move the manipulatives as they create their literary models. At the sharing stage, they walk around and listen to explanations of their peers. Thus, movement is natural; and teachers benefit by harnessing this natural energy instead of fighting it (Hecker, 1997). The use of manipulatives, however, engages the brain's other systems, as well.

Hands-on learning stimulates the *emotional* learning system because students think working with manipulatives is fun, and building models of what they read is an extension of play. Manipulatives activate the *cognitive* learning system because students must understand what they read to build a model of it, and they must think how best to represent words and ideas with colorful, three-dimensional objects. If they work with a partner or in a small group, they involve the *social* learning system. Together, they process information, share ideas, discuss, negotiate, compromise, cooperate, and collaborate to complete the task at hand. They offer suggestions and defend their positions; and when they explain their model, students use "we" instead of "I," because they recognize it as a group effort.

Manipulatives offer opportunities for two kinds of *reflective* learning: ongoing and after-the-fact. As students build their models, they are constantly reflecting on whether the model shows what they want it to show; revision is instantaneous and continuous. When the model is complete, students reflect on the process (why they built the model the way they did), the product (what the model shows), and their learning (what they learned from building the model).

Coaching Students

Teachers can *coach* and inspire students in the management of the brain's physical learning system just as basketball coaches inspire clumsy adolescents to develop grace on the court. For example, teacher-*coaches* identify what students do well and then build on those skills for greater accomplishments. Teachers can ask questions like these about students' models or other manipulatives:

> ➤ In your model, you captured two of the three themes from the novel. How might you show the third?

➤ The vocabulary cards you made helped you get a high score on the test. Would you like to make a Flip Chute or Task Cards for learning the state capitals?

Teacher-*coaches* are alert to students who tend to "live" in their physical learning systems while ignoring other aspects of their lives. When the *need to do* is satisfied with sport, dance, drama, or other socially acceptable engagements, limited growth in the other systems may be overlooked. School "stars," for example, may be encouraged to devote the bulk of their waking hours to physical practice by adults who unwittingly approve of limited attention to balanced development of all five systems. This is unfortunate, because each system contributes to a well-rounded individual.

Further, when students rely predominantly on physical stimulation to obtain a sense of self, they may graduate from rough-and-tumble sport to higher levels of physical stimulation that produce a rush of adrenaline and "feel good" brain chemicals. When the brain's other learning systems are underdeveloped and legitimate activity no longer produces the sought-after chemical result, students—or adults—may turn to alcohol, drugs, and sexual activity as illegitimate stimulants for the physical system. Teacher-coaches, therefore, must inspire their students to channel physical energies into worthwhile activities for personal and academic growth while also attending to growth in the other systems—especially the reflective system, because it helps students gain a realistic sense of self.

6

The Reflective Learning System

hereas the brain's physical learning system is the oldest and most primitive system, the reflective learning system is the most sophisticated, even though it was the last to develop in terms of evolution; it is the last to fully develop within one's lifetime. Reflective learning deals with the brain and body's executive functions, such as higher-level thinking and problem solving. In the present, it mentally relives the past while contemplating the future. Some scientists say it is this system that distinguishes us from chimpanzees and other apes and makes us human (Dozier, 1998; Restak, 1994).

In his book *Outsmarting IQ*, David Perkins (1995), senior research associate at the Harvard Graduate School of Education, defines *mindfulness* as the artful use of the mind—monitoring one's own thinking, trying to manage thinking in effective ways. These overall metacognitive functions of thinking are the basis of what he referred to as *reflective intelligence*. When we nurture this intelligence and purposely develop it, Perkins says, the reflective system allows us to become all we are capable of becoming (Figure 6.1). He calls this learnable, acquired aspect of who we are *mindware;* it is "whatever people can learn that helps them to solve problems, make decisions, understand difficult concepts, and perform other intellectually demanding tasks better" (p. 13). Mindfulness and reflective thinking require nurturing; they do represent learnable intelligence. Yet, in a blistering indictment, Perkins expresses grave concern about the lack of adequate attention to teaching reflective thought:

Hardly anything in conventional educational practice promotes, in a direct and straightforward way, thoughtfulness and the use of strategies to guide thinking. Those students who acquire reflective intelligence build it on their own, by working out personal repertoires of strategies. Or they pick it up from the home environment, where some parents more than others model good reasoning in dinner table conversation, press their children to think out decisions, emphasize the importance of a systematic approach to school work, and so on. (p. 117)

Similarly, Damasio (1999) refers to a biologically complex phenomenon called *extended consciousness,* which evolves throughout one's lifetime as a result of experience. Though this definition is descriptively similar to Perkins' learnable *reflective*

—FIGURE 6.1—

THE REFLECTIVE LEARNING SYSTEM WORKS BEST WHEN TAUGHT REFLECTIVE STRATEGIES

**Efforts to Enhance Reflective Thinking
and Learning and Avoid Potholes of Cognition**

- Take time to problem solve; gather comprehensive evidence; avoid hasty judgments.
- Foster open-mindedness to see past own position and beliefs that promote self-interest.
- Consider objections and alternative views objectively.
- Generate multiple interpretations and perspectives before decision making.
- Interrupt automatic behaviors and reconsider habitual acts.
- Remember, each person sees the same thing through the lens of personal experience.
- Draw inferences from readings.
- Develop well-organized persuasive arguments in writing.
- Strive to paraphrase key concepts in science and mathematics.
- Look for and think in patterns.
- Recognize efforts to rationalize thoughts and behaviors.
- Entertain alternative view to one's own narrow (my side is the right side) thinking.
- Clarify fuzzy, imprecise, unclear thinking.
- Recognize thinking that *sprawls* across content unnecessarily.
- Maintain a positive attitude toward thinking, self-monitoring and regulation, use of decision-making strategies, and exploration into possibilities.

Source: Data from Perkins, D. (1995). *Outsmarting IQ: The emerging science of learnable intelligence.* New York: The Free Press, p. 146

intelligence and *mindware,* Damasio believes that extended consciousness displays knowledge to enable intelligent processing to occur. He argues, however, that extended consciousness is not intelligence. In this chapter, I rely on both Perkins' concept of *mindware* and Damasio's concept of *extended consciousness* to describe the reflective learning system. In addition, to promote an in-depth understanding of the reflective learning system, I discuss conscience and spirit, stages of reflective learning, and metacognitive learning strategies that help strengthen the reflective learning system.

The Basis of Reflective Learning

Extended consciousness allows us to become known to ourselves. It prompts development of an "autobiographical self" that permits us to make the most of a situation, because it includes the ability to analyze facts, identify discords in the search for truth, build norms and ideals for behavior, and use memory, reasoning, and language to creatively generate new ideas and artifacts (Damasio, 1999).

Damasio (1999) declares that *extended consciousness,* from his perspective, goes beyond the foundational core consciousness of the here and now; extended consciousness includes thought processes that allow contemplation of historical perspectives and anticipation of the future. In contrast, *core consciousness* refers to *feelings* of nonverbal knowing that occur when we see, hear, touch, smell, or taste something that creates a visual, auditory, olfactory, or visceral feeling identified as *temporary knowledge,* either actual or recalled. The core sense of self is built on these feelings of core consciousness, whereas extended consciousness goes beyond the core by involving implicit memories (see Chapter 4) that we can recall and reconstruct.

This higher level of consciousness extends the sense of self to personal likes, dislikes, and individual identity, based on historically rich memories of the past, a sense of ourselves in the present, and a glimpse of who we might become in an anticipated future; all these are subject to change with experience. According to Damasio (1999), higher-order extended consciousness develops the individual, as reflection influences our imagination of what might have been and what might be. Extended consciousness allows us to be curious about the self, which leads to the development of our *conscience.*

Conscience and the Human Spirit

The human conscience permits us to develop a sense of right and wrong, good and evil, and a feeling for where our actions fall along these continuums. The exercise of one's conscience creates personal *spirit*—an attitude of life that mediates between the mind and body. A person's spirit manifests as temperament and personality of the emotional system, yet it is deeper and more pervasive than what other people can observe. Spirit is our internal code of conduct, a pervasive energy, zeal, essence, personal drive, and enterprise. The conscience, or our spiritual self, monitors our feelings, thoughts, and actions and attempts to keep them congruent with our deeply held beliefs about self and others. These are all basic to the reflective learning system.

As students mature, they bring along their slowly evolved moral discipline—their spirit—now deeply embedded within their being. That moral development guides their work ethic, their sense of fairness, and their personal commitment to promote a healthy society or to engage in its demise. How societies guide the development of children's reflective learning systems, therefore, will make the difference between healthful versus damaging lifestyles of their citizens and ultimately the success or downfall of society.

Neurobiological Basis of Reflective Learning

Reflective learning depends on basic input from our senses and internal viscera, as well as complex memory systems, numerous brain structures, pathways, networks, and subsystems. These brain systems include subsystems associated with the cerebellum, hypothalamus, thalamus, hippocampus, sensory association areas, and frontal and prefrontal cortices. The frontal lobes, however, are perhaps the most critical for reflective learning; yet they cannot function properly unless the basic core systems are intact.

Our frontal and prefrontal cortices act as massive inhibitors and shapers of primary urges, such as aggression, violence, and sexual activity. These lobes allow us to do the following:

➤ Anticipate future consequences of our actions.
➤ Develop plans and goals.
➤ Work toward goal accomplishment.
➤ Balance and control our emotions.

➤ Maintain a sense of ourselves as active contributors toward our future well-being.

During the past 2.5 million years, the human brain quadrupled in size; the areas of greatest expansion were the frontal lobes—especially that portion under the forehead called the *prefrontal cortex*. These lobes comprise almost 40 percent of the total cortical area of the brain and are more than 200 percent larger than the chimpanzee brain (Dozier, 1998; Restak, 1994). As one might expect, their size is in direct proportion to human functions *un*available to other animals (Restak).

Science writer Rush Dozier, Jr. (1998) speculates that the enlarged frontal lobes evolved as powerful monitoring and control mechanisms to combat our powerful fears and primitive urges. Thus, the reflective learning system of the frontal lobes wields an executive control function to prevent spontaneous eruption of primitive urges and emotional outbursts through intentional, learned responses.

Although frontal lobes of our left and the right hemispheres have differing functions, their overall tasks—in addition to controlling primitive urges—include the following:

➤ Organizing.
➤ Scheduling.
➤ Motivating.
➤ Sticking with tasks.
➤ Anticipating future consequences of present actions.
➤ Being aware of oneself in terms of successes and failures.
➤ Coordinating the necessary steps to complete a task or to achieve a goal.
➤ Monitoring what one says and does.
➤ Analyzing past thoughts and behaviors.
➤ Projecting into the future.
➤ Empathizing.
➤ Establishing expectations (Dozier, 1998).

Perhaps of greatest importance, the frontal lobes tell us what *not* to say and do (Diamond, personal communication). Their ongoing development, therefore, is vitally important for keeping us out of trouble. Unfortunately, Restak (1994) and other cognitive scientists fear that the frontal lobes of many youth today are going underdeveloped and appear damaged.

Frontal Lobe Damage

Neuropsychologist Donald Stuss and neurologist Frank Benson (1992) identify five major frontal lobe malfunctions that affect reflection and learning:

1. Loss of ambition and self-motivated behavior that produces lethargy and apathy.

2. Sequencing disturbances that create difficulties in keeping track of information and separating essential information from background material.

3. Lack of executive control that results in disrupted ability to plan and anticipate the consequences of one's own behavior.

4. A disturbed future memory capability that interferes with goal setting and comparing today's achievement with anticipated accomplishments.

5. A disruption in the sense of self-continuity from past into the future that causes failure to see one's self as an evolving person and diminishes personal responsibility.

"People with frontal lobe damage typically perseverate on old strategies and do not plan ahead effectively. They are susceptible to living within the present moment, in a more animal-like state of existence" (Panksepp, 1998, p. 316). Damage to the frontal lobes—dependent on the location—can create almost as much difficulty as severing the nerve fibers. For example, Restak (1994) reports:

> Injury to the orbital frontal cortex along the underside produces impulsivity, rapid mood changes, irritability, and sometimes physical aggression. If the injury is to the lateral parts of the frontal lobes, the person loses all initiative and spontaneity; the mood is flat and disengaged; initiative is replaced by inertia and a "couldn't care less" attitude. Although these two forms of frontal lobe disturbance seem quite different, they share a basic failure in regulating conduct and behavior in accordance with either social convention or internal goals. (pp. 99–100)

Other side effects of frontal lobe damage include difficulties with working memory; loss of verbal spontaneity; discontinued play; violence, aggression, and fear; disaggregation of the personality; failure to integrate experiences; a shift to boastful, uninhibited speech; and lack of concern for work, family, or the future (Greenfield, 1997; Restak, 1994). Susan Greenfield, professor of pharmacology at Oxford University and professor of physics at Gresham College in London, concludes that when patients had damage to their frontal lobe areas, it was almost as if they lacked the "inner resources that act for most of us as shock absorbers to the happenstance of life" (p. 21).

Based on frontal lobe studies, neurologists conclude that damage can interfere with self-monitoring of ongoing behavior and the ability to alter it in response to positive or negative feedback; thus, erratic impulsive acts take full reign (Dozier, 1998). Frontal lobe damage can seriously diminish a person's capacity to empathize with others; without this essential ability, remorse is not possible nor is a sense of fairness or forgiveness of others (Restak, 1994).

These are serious consequences of frontal lobe damage; yet at one time, scientists thought the frontal lobes were of little importance because they did not respond to electrical stimulation (Restak, 1994). In fact, Greenfield (1997) reports that between 1935 and 1978, 35,000 people in the United States underwent a *prefrontal lobotomy*—the surgical procedure discussed earlier—that cut the nerve fibers connecting the frontal lobes to the rest of the brain. When one considers the dramatic side effects, it seems odd that so many operations were performed to relieve patients of depression, anxiety, phobias, and aggression without clear awareness of the devastating impact of the procedure. At that time, however, physicians thought the detrimental effects were minimal, despite the profound changes in the patients.

Surprisingly, severe frontal lobe damage can appear to have no effect on intellectual functioning in terms of language, perception, or other cognitive processes, even though the frontal lobes have massive networks of connecting fibers with all parts of the brain (Damasio, 1994; Restak, 1994). Patients can clearly state what they "should" do, but be unable to execute those behaviors. Further, without the regulating power of the frontal lobes, language and cognitive functions fail to produce the kinds of thinking and behavior patterns necessary for successful living.

I have often observed adolescents in alternative education classes sit listlessly one moment and explode in a flurry of insults the next. I wonder if Restak's (1994) warning is not already on us. He writes:

We have learned that our knowledge of the frontal lobes provides a new way of looking at important and puzzling social dysfunction. If the frontal lobes are not nurtured and developed in portions of our population . . . then we as a society can expect to continue to pay dearly in terms of more crime, broken homes, drug use, and violence. (pp. 108–109).

Because the frontal lobes continue to develop through adolescence and into adulthood, educators continue to have opportunities for making a difference in students considered difficult to teach, as well as those whose stages of development are within expectations.

Stages of Reflective Learning

Erik Erikson (1982), an influential psychologist who described stages of personality development, believed that humans have a built-in drive to acquire increasingly complex learning systems in an age-appropriate fashion, even though some people get stuck along the way. He identified stages of development that may be used as guides for helping children develop insights into their own thinking (see Figure 6.2). Even though Erikson's stages are based on general, metaphorical, and descriptive grounds, rather than on scientific validation, recent research suggests that these stages reflect normal development of the frontal lobes and that they are appropriate for designing various levels of reflective learning strategies and metacognitive instruction (Borich & Tombari, 1997).

Trust Versus Mistrust

According to Erikson (1982), the usual outcome of each bipolar stage, such as *trust* versus *mistrust,* is to emerge with a combination of the two extremes. Sometimes the combination is positive, and sometimes it is negative. In the case of *trust* versus *mistrust,* the emerging positive quality is *hope;* negative outcomes are *doubt* and *uncertainty* about one's emerging autobiographical self. Thus, as a child completes the first two years of life, she is expected to reflect a positive, trusting outlook of *hope.* If, however, the child experiences early deprivation, neglect, or mistreatment, then mistrust and a negative, "misbehaving" toddler results. Although a rich and stimulating environment is best, researchers recently reported that doubt and confusion can be overcome during the next stage of a child's life when provided an abundance of loving care and nurturing (Sprinthall, Sprinthall, & Oja, 1994).

—*FIGURE 6.2*—

ERIKSON'S EIGHT STAGES OF PSYCHOSOCIAL/PERSONALITY DEVELOPMENT

Stage (Approximate Age)	Qualities Involved	Positive Outcome	Activities Associated with This Stage
Oral-sensory (Birth to age 6 years)	Trust versus mistrust	Hope	Trust in caregiver for developing a secure attachment.
Muscular-anal (Ages 2 to 3 years)	Autonomy versus shame and doubt	Will	Learns to walk, grasp, control toileting; exerts self as a person.
Locomotor (Ages 4 to 5 years)	Initiative versus guilt	Purpose	Works toward self-directed goals; identifies with like-sex parent.
Latency (Ages 6 to 12 years)	Mastery versus inferiority	Competence	Develops academic and social skills.
Adolescence (Ages 13 to 18 years)	Identity versus role confusion	Fidelity	Faithful to self-image; achieves sexual identity; searches for new values.
Young adulthood (Ages 19 to 25 years)	Intimacy versus isolation		Forms one or more intimate relationships; may marry.
Middle adulthood (Ages 26 to 40 years)	Generativity versus stagnation		Raises family; focuses on work and creativity.
Maturity (40+ years)	Ego integrity versus despair		Integrates prior stages; accepts basic identity; accepts self.

Source: Data from Bee, H. (1995). *The Developing Child,* 7th ed. (p. 277). New York: HarperCollins and Sprinthall, N., Sprinthall, R., & Oja, S. (1994). *Educational Psychology,* 6th ed. (pp. 145–160). New York: McGraw-Hill, Inc.

Autonomy Versus Shame and Doubt

Between 2 and 3 years of age, children develop *personal will* through the resolution of conflicts between a desire for *self-direction* ("I want to do it myself!") and *shame and doubt* resulting from punishment when exploring the environment. Many situations can depress the child's opportunities to develop a comfortable sense of self, or what Erikson called *personal will,* such as harsh punishment for "getting into things," punitive bowel training methods, an overemphasis on "No," doing for the child what he is attempting to do alone—such as tying shoes—instead of guiding him to do it alone, limited language stimulation, and overprotection.

By contrast, children become self-directed, develop initial independence, and learn to think for themselves when caretakers do the following:

> Ask thought-provoking questions ("What will happen if I pour all the water from the big glass into the little cup?").

> Engage the child in work and conversation ("Would you help me put the blocks on the shelf?").

> Give the child clear, acceptable choices ("Would you like to use the red crayon or the blue one?").

> Replace the parental "No" with mediating comments that help the child understand what is to be done and why ("Let's close the door to keep out the cold" or "Take my hand when we cross the street so a car won't hit you").

> Orally label things in the environment ("That is a truck, a big dump truck that hauls gravel").

The outcome of a child's desire for independence (autonomy), combined with self-restraint (sense of shame or doubt for disobeying), is what Erikson referred to as *will*—not willfulness, but *personal will* or determination to become an independent person.

Initiative Versus Guilt

During the third stage of childhood development, according to this theory, children develop *purpose* and a sense of sexual identity as they imitate the parent of the same sex and vie for the affections of the opposite-sex parent. A 5-year-old boy may say that when he grows up he will never marry so he can stay home and take care of his mother. A girl may say she wants to go in the car with Daddy while Mother stays home. If punished or ridiculed for these innocent remarks, children may develop strong feelings of guilt about their identity. Parents who reassure their children that they will grow up to be full-fledged adults and wonderful parents—probably even better than the parents they have—help them develop a firm foundation for the next stage of personal development while they gain a sense of sexual identity.

During this stage, many children attend preschool and kindergarten. Sprinthall and colleagues (1994) reported on a longitudinal investigation of children at this stage, in which the Brookline Early Education Program (BEEP) studied nearly 300 children and their parents by comparing two approaches to early childhood education in comparison to a group receiving no specific intervention. One group enjoyed a Piagetian, child-centered program that varied the amount of structure and support, in accord with developmental needs of the children. The children's parents also participated in training, according to their level of parenting skill. The program for another group of children was oriented toward academic achievement reinforced with behavior-modification techniques.

Children in the Piagetian, child-centered group far outperformed children in the other two groups in both academic and social performance. Children identified as high risk for school failure at the initiation of the study made the greatest gains, while others in this group had fewer academic failures and fewer referrals for behavior difficulties 12 years later.

In contrast, children's initiative and competence in the behavior-modification program were actually depressed. Twelve years later, these children demonstrated higher rates of behavior problems and delinquency in school (Schweinhart, Weikart, & Larner, cited in Sprinthall et al., 1994). It became obvious that when children were educated according to developmental stages, internal versus external controls emerged as children developed *purpose* in their lives by balancing initiative with guilt.

Mastery Versus Inferiority

From 6 to 12 years of age, children work through the *mastery versus inferiority* stage as they struggle to develop *competence* with schoolwork and with peer interactions. They are generally eager to learn; and they think it is fun to decipher words, learn to write, and compute. As they develop skills, they also develop a sense of personal mastery in school, on the playground, and in activities with friends. They generally prefer working and playing with same-gender classmates, but they can successfully work in mixed-gender cooperative groups. Their energy levels are high, and they require a curriculum that allows them ample opportunity for physical movement.

At this stage, children have an inborn drive to master their environment; and elementary teachers are in a strategic position to emphasize activities that nurture—and in many cases, restore—children's sense of mastery while strengthening reflective learning. Unfortunately, many children fail to obtain a satisfactory level of personal mastery in school, so they search for it on the streets, in gangs, or hidden away in their bedrooms searching the Internet. In 1992 Randall Jones studied more than 500 children in grades 3 and 4 and found that during a five-month period, about one-fourth of them had been involved in drug abuse (cigarettes, smokeless tobacco, alcohol, glue, marijuana, or cocaine). Psychosocial results for these youngsters on Erikson's rating scale revealed low scores on earlier stages of *trust* and *industry,* whereas their nonabusing peers gained on all measures, as expected. Jones's study underscores the importance of frontal lobe nurturance.

During the mastery stage, children can develop strategies of metacognitive thought. They can learn to keep simple graphs of their academic progress, and they can conduct experiments to determine under what types of conditions they learn best: with bright light or dim; with music in the background or when it is quiet; working alone, with someone else, or in a small group. They can experiment to determine if they learn best when they see, hear, touch, or move the material to be learned. Recordkeeping gives them concrete evidence of their progress, and it can go a long way in helping them gain a sense of mastery. All children need to feel successful for the promotion of personal industry and mastery; and they should be engaged in *doing* far more than in listening. As with the brain's physical learning system, concrete learning is excellent preparation for reflective learning, which can flower during the adolescent stage.

Elementary students can begin giving conscious attention to their reflective learning systems by developing self-monitoring strategies and ongoing recordkeeping systems of their skill development. We can teach students to ask themselves questions like these:

> What helped me remember the most information: drawing it on flip cards, acting it out, or hearing a story about it?
> If I work alone, will I remember more than when I work with others?

We must explicitly teach such strategies because children as young as ages 5 to 7 are capable of thinking metacognitively. But they may fail to notice that the strategy is helping them and thus not think to use it in similar circumstances later (Pressley cited in Borich & Tombari, 1997). Research on classroom instruction in strategies makes it clear that children as young as 2nd grade can regulate their use of cognitive strategies so long as they have systematic instruction in doing so.

Borich and Tombari (1997) report on studies involving 5th and 6th graders who demonstrated the ability to remember and use two strategies for vocabulary words. Interestingly, the students failed to notice that one strategy was more effective than the other. Once this was pointed out to them, they chose to use the more effective strategy on their academic road to competence.

Identity Versus Role Confusion

From about 13 to 18 years of age, youngsters think about things in terms of subjective perceptions and objective realities, particularly in terms of their own identity. For example, they can differentiate feelings and emotions in themselves and others. They can assume the perspective of another person, understand symbolic meaning, and role-play "as-if" scenarios. Walking in the shoes of another, so to speak, helps them develop empathy and altruism.

Though adolescents are capable of role-playing and empathy, David Elkind (1978) warns that these emerging capabilities tend to be overwhelming toward the beginning of this stage. Then, adolescents are self-absorbed and ego-centric—certain that everyone is focused on them, that everyone else notices their appearance and behavior, and that no one could possibly understand them. They invent imaginary audiences to whom they play out their deep-rooted belief in their personal uniqueness. Adolescents invent stories about themselves and begin to identify with what they invent.

I cannot overstate the power of adolescents' invented audiences and imaginary stories about themselves. During this time in their lives, youngsters rely on all previous effective accomplishments to develop a strong sense of autobiographical identity—for now and for their imagined future. If, for example, a student is still operating at a *mistrust* level and has not yet developed initiative and *mastery,* then the audience and the stories can become all too real to them; and the adolescent remains confused and unable to cope with social and physical changes.

The horrific shootings at Columbine High School and at other middle and high schools across the United States poignantly illustrate how easy it is for adolescents to act out their invented stories to invoke an imagined audience reaction. "They'll see we're not afraid of them!" "They think they're big shots. Wait 'til they see who's a big shot!" "Jocks think they're tough guys. We'll show them who's tough!"

Contrast these self-absorbed negative scenarios with others that tend to be more positive: "Everyone thinks I'm handsome. The girls will drool when they see me in my new jacket." "My friends think I write well. They'll think I'm really cool when I'm chosen yearbook editor."

Students strongly desire affiliation and identity with a group of peers and authentic feelings of competence within the group, as discussed in Chapter 3. When achieved, a sense of *fidelity* to the group emerges. When competence and affiliation are not achieved, students are apt to fantasize how to "get even," and since their fantasies appear real, they are more prone to act on them.

Students at this age pay vastly more attention to what peers say and what they imagine peers think than they do to what parents, relatives, and least of all, teachers say. Battles between teachers and adolescents can become heated with anger, disappointment, and emotional pain as adolescents fail to complete their homework, leave messes in the lab, fail to respond when asked to participate, and engage in antisocial behaviors. Teachers must refrain from nagging; rather, they must assess the circumstances and determine alternative ways of reaching a child rather than through confrontation. As Barbara Coloroso (1989), author of the video and audio tape *Winning at Teaching...without beating your kids* and other works in the *Kids Are Worth It!* series, repeatedly advises that unless the situation is life-threatening or morally wrong, "allow children to experience the real world consequences for their own irresponsibility" (p. 35).

Teachers who recognize characteristics of this stage develop nonlecturing curricula—even curricula based on state-mandated learning standards—that focus on helping students understand themselves and others without lecturing. For example, Coloroso finds that "minilectures" provide information students already know or do not care to hear: "If you'd have put your coat on, you wouldn't be cold." "If you hadn't hit her, you wouldn't be in the office." "If you'd have studied, you wouldn't have failed."

During this stage, students are able to intentionally develop metacognitive skills that take advantage of their self-absorption and their personal changes. This development assumes, of course, that they have mastered previous stages, including some skill in self-assessment. Throughout the middle and high school grades, students' ability to engage in a kind of self-reflection shifts to thinking about their own thinking and the thinking of others. This is an ideal time to pose imaginative scenarios to prompt internal dialogues that rely on the use of memory strategies. At this age, students can become aware of and consciously monitor and control their thinking. Thus, they can meaningfully engage in *metacognition*.

Students can learn to use learning strategies and pick and choose among them, but not until they do so deliberately are they engaged in a metacognitive process. For instance, when a student summarizes a chapter, he is using a learning strategy. When he purposefully constructs a summary to reflect on his understanding of the material, he is employing metacognition (Bondy, cited in Sprinthall et al., 1994).

Adult Stages

The next three Eriksonian stages—young adulthood (ages 19 to 25), middle adulthood (ages 26 to 40), and maturity (ages 40 plus)—refer to adults. Teachers would do well to engage in some self-analysis to determine where on the scale they fall and then make plans to work through any "stuck" points. Without question, to be effective, teachers need to understand themselves even better than they understand their students. If teachers feel deprived of an intimate relationship, they may expect interactions with students to provide a sense of being needed and loved. Forget it! Teachers are supposed to attend to the needs of students, not to expect teaching to cure their psychosocial difficulties.

Teachers may get in a rut and stagnate after teaching for a few years. Investment in exciting workshops, conferences, and school-community service projects with their students can help turn that feeling around. While working with teachers instructing severely troubled youth, I see many teachers fall into despair and lose their sense of identity as excellent teachers when students continue to create trouble for themselves and others. Every few years, teachers are encouraged to alternate their teaching assignments to avoid falling into these "teacher burnout" traps.

To foster ongoing comfort with the teaching profession, we need to remember that students like to work with teachers who are trustworthy, fair, and concerned. They want teachers to be experts in what they are teaching, and they expect them to care about their students so they can talk with teachers about their concerns. Teachers who are both respected and liked generate student satisfaction and academic achievement. Teachers who think about their own thinking are in a good position to teach students how to consider *their* thinking.

Educating Students in Reflective Learning

Of all the brain's systems, the ability to reflect is the one most critically in need of thoughtful attention; it helps control and mediate all other systems, and it makes the difference between socially appropriate and inappropriate behaviors. It is the system that allows us to become all we are capable of becoming emotionally, socially, cognitively, physically, and metacognitively. When unattended and left to develop without conscious monitoring and direction, this system fails as a controlling system and allows impulsivity, aggression, violence, sexual abuse, lack of remorse and self-assessment, and other antisocial behavior to emerge.

Frontal lobe functioning is so much a part of who we are that we often fail to appreciate the complexities involved, and we may unwittingly fail to promote its effective development. For example, learning experiences during infancy and the preschool years prompt rapid cell growth at a time when caregivers tend to provide rich sensory stimulation. A growth spurt occurs again at approximately 11 years of age when preadolescents have an opportunity to personally guide development of their learning (Giedd, 2000). During this time, youngsters can challenge their brains with a huge amount of socially acceptable or socially unacceptable experiences, or they can let the opportunity for brain development pass them by as they shuffle through life in a passive or antisocial way.

To reverse the trend toward antisocial behaviors by a growing segment of the adolescent population, educators need to focus on frontal lobe development. Also, media and corporate executives, as well as politicians, should consider the effect of their products and programs on the emerging development of children's conscience.

Metacognition

In the 1970s, a Russian psychologist, A. R. Luria (1973), described the use of self-talk to regulate one's behavior. He observed that prefrontal cortical damage often created impulsive behavior, explosive anger, and fear. He also found that students who behaved as if suffering frontal lobe damage could be taught to use self-talk to curb their impulsive acts and function appropriately. Because the reflective learning system allows humans to carry on dialogues in their heads and invent audiences and personal stories for self-glorification, we can try out ideas, rethink interactions, and project future results of some proposed action without actually engaging in it. This allows us to cultivate thinking strategies and attitudes we can use to control genetic predispositions that do not serve us well. Further, it allows us to challenge ourselves to higher levels of skill development and personal accomplishment through the cultivation of self-monitoring and personal management habits. The key word here is *cultivation*, because we must nurture reflective learning throughout our lives to prevent its damage and to maximize its strategic power as the mind's chief executive officer (CEO).

As far as we know, humans are the only creatures with the ability to analyze their thoughts and behavior and then act in accordance with expectations for goal attainment. No other species can keep careful records of their behavior and critically analyze those records to determine patterns of activity over time, whether those patterns pertain to weight loss, the number of math problems solved, or the shift in an attitude toward others. No other creatures engage in thinking about their own thinking and engage in management of their cognitive functioning.

As Albert Ellis, the father of rational emotive therapy, said in 1973, humans are remarkably complex, cognitive-emotive-behaving creatures. Of mankind's main traits, Ellis said,

> his high-level ability to think—especially his ability to think about his thinking—is probably his most unique and most "human" quality. If, therefore, he is to work effectively against his strong individual and societal tendencies to "dehumanize" himself, he had better learn to employ vigorously some of the highest-level thinking and metathinking of which he is innately capable but which he easily neglects and avoids. (pp. 3–4)

Learning Strategies

A strategy is a clever plan or action for accomplishing a task by making it easier or more effective. The word *strategy* is borrowed from the military and, when combined with *tactic,* another military term that refers to a planned action for a specific purpose, it becomes immediately applicable to teaching. Thus, a student may use a single learning strategy to locate important information, enhance reading comprehension, arrange new information so it can be remembered, recall steps of the writing process, and so forth. You can teach students a strategy as a separate skill before applying it to course content (Deshler & Schumaker, 1988), but integrating several strategies into a comprehensive, composite approach applied directly to new learning can dramatically reduce the time it takes to learn the strategy while increasing the amount of meaningful information learned (Given, 1991, 1994).

An integrated-strategies approach to learning provides an excellent metacognitive or self-talk guide. The important teaching consideration when using strategies is to remember that you need to teach students reflective thinking and metacognition deliberately, in a consistent manner, until students internalize the process. Then they can mix and match strategies to reflect on any circumstances.

Over a five-year period, I developed a comprehensive set of language arts learning strategies that graduate students and I implemented with children, adolescents, and adults who were identified as underachieving or learning disabled. Each summer we collected data, made improvements, and then taught the strategies the following summer in their revised form (Given, 1991, 1994). The integrated sets of strategies that evolved are called ACT and PRAISES. (Figures 6.3 and 6.4 portray the primary components of this integrated-strategies model that spell out the acronym.) Note that individual strategies in the model associate with one or more of the natural learning systems covered in this text: For example, "Inform with Paraphrase" focuses on oral communications basic to the social learning system; "Self-monitor and Review" reflects metacognition and self-analysis of the reflective learning system; "Arrange to Remember" gives the physical learning system an active role for learning.

In a six-week period, spending three hours per day, we found that students at all ages were able to learn the strategies at varying levels of sophistication. Students in 2nd through 5th grades concentrated on the major headings of ACT and PRAISES (e.g., Assume Responsibility, Consider What I Know, Preview Main Ideas, etc.), which are the basic acronym (Given, 1991, 1994). Students from 6th grade through adulthood either focused on this basic level or expanded their strategic approach to include subcomponents to guide their behavior for skill development.

During the last summer I directed the program, my colleagues and I compared our data with implementation results from the University of Kansas Strategies

---

—FIGURE 6.3—

COGNITIVE ACROSTICS: PROMPTS FOR LEARNING—ACT

ACT: Getting Ready to Learn

Dates												
Assume responsibility.	(Check when strategy is implemented.)											
Arrive prepared.												
Build a personal plan.												
Listen to positive self-talk.												
Engage enthusiastically.												
Consider what I know.												
Describe the concept or topic.												
Examine personal and vicarious experiences.												
Clarify characteristics and descriptions.												
List examples, non- & sometimes examples.												
Announce how it works or functions.												
Recall associations and implications.												
Explore metaphors and modifications.												
Target my goal.												
Assess the task.												
Crystallize expected achievement.												
Embark: begin the learning adventure.												

Source: From "Operation Breakthrough for Continuous Self-Systems Improvement" by B. K. Given, 1994, *Intervention 30, 1,* pp. 38–46. Copyright 1994 by PRO-ED, Inc. Adapted with permission.

Intervention Model (SIM), where instructors taught one strategy at a time with material unrelated to course content (Deshler & Schumaker, 1988). We found that our students learned and applied three or more strategies with the same percentage of success in the same time frame that SIM students learned and applied one strategy. Further, because our students developed the strategies to enhance their understanding of information read, there was no need for them to transfer skills learned in isolation to authentic material later. The value of a comprehensive-strategies approach is that it offers a package of integrated strategies to remember rather than a host of unrelated strategies. In both cases, however, students required ongoing support for using the strategies on their own and for applying them across settings (Deshler & Schumaker, 1988; Given, 1991).

—FIGURE 6.4—

COGNITIVE ACROSTICS: PROMPTS FOR LEARNING—PRAISES

PRAISES for Interactive Learning

Dates										

Preview and map main ideas.

Motivate reading: photo-read.										
Analyze illustrations, captions, questions										
Produce idea maps.										

Read for meaning.

Review for clues.										
Enter list items if useful.										
Accept list items if parallel.										
Defend heading if separate and short.										
Save non-list details on prompt cards.										

Arrange to remember.

Organize ideas on a mind map.										
Role-play new learning through story.										
Draw pictures as mnemonics.										
Erect meaning with dioramas, mobiles, etc.										
Respond alone or with others.										

Inform with paraphrase.

Tell a story or use rap, rhythm, or rhyme.										
Ask if the message is clear.										
Listen for meaning.										
Keep comments on track.										

Script to communicate.

Write topic sentences from map or diagram.										
Restate concepts using lists and cards.										
Include metaphors and analogies.										
Think of a conclusion.										
Examine for accuracy and clarity.										

Edit for errors.

Evaluate noun-verb agreement.										
Develop a variety of sentence patterns.										
Investigate written mechanics.										
Take time to revise, rewrite, and share.										

Self-monitor with pride.

Ponder record of progress.										
Reflect on goals.										
Identify how to use new learning.										
Determine ways to increase progress.										
Establish expectations for improvement.										

Source: From "Operation Breakthrough for Continuous Self-Systems Improvement" by B. K. Given, 1994, *Intervention 30, 1,* pp. 38–46. Copyright 1994 by PRO-ED, Inc. Adapted with permission.

Educational Considerations

Reflective learning is the system that monitors activities of all other brain systems and manages them, just as an executive manages a complex corporation. An effective executive empowers others to take responsibility for specific jobs, and she keeps close tabs on how well workers execute their duties and then intervenes, as needed, with guiding, nurturing interactions for the benefit of the company.

Understanding the Teacher's Role

In classrooms, teachers can assume the role of an effective executive who empowers students to reach for their highest goals. The executive teacher serves as a steward who teaches students strategies for beneficial expenditure of their resources. She guides students toward higher-order thinking to generate insights into their thoughts and actions, and to generate energy and power for changing their individual minds and learning something new.

Just as CEOs of corporations are decision makers, so too are teachers. They collect and analyze data to determine what works well and what needs to be modified, deleted, or continued. They reflect on their findings to predict future outcomes. The classroom executive uses performance-based assessment, such as portfolios, journals, projects, conference notes, and other authentic procedures, and she models evaluative questioning so students learn how to critique and assess their work both subjectively and objectively. The role of the executive is to prepare students to reflect on their thoughts, behaviors, and beliefs and make decisions based on evidence and judgment. The executive teacher teaches students strategies for learning and thinking about one's own thinking. In the multiplex information-processing model presented in Chapter 4, reflective learning is the construction and reconstruction of knowledge and beliefs, with reconstruction based on self-reflection representing the highest cognitive ability.

Perkins (1995) suggests that the brain's reflective system has responsibility for bucking the trend of what the mind may wish to do. It harnesses the mind and forces it to break out of its typical ruts of thinking, to go beyond genetically predisposed urges and concrete experiences, and to think about *how* one thinks as well as *what* one thinks. According to Csikszentmihalyi (1990), when we make the shift to reflective thought and cognitive self-control, we should recognize that consciousness is not entirely controlled by its biological programming but is self-directed. This statement underscores the concept that the brain's reflective learning system is the control mechanism for extended consciousness, as defined by Damasio (1999).

Keeping the Reflective Learning System in Balance

The reflective learning system has a strong *need to experiment and explore,* and teachers who *guide* that exploration help students reflect on past emotions, interactions, thoughts, ideas, and behavior and consider them in relation to what is happening today. Teacher-*guides* or *executives* also serve as talent scouts who identify and highlight student strengths that may otherwise go unnoticed. They encourage students to contemplate how they are growing across the systems and how current sensations and experiences might affect the future.

The major role of the teacher-guide is to foster metacognitive thought, so students take responsibility for their actions and understand how the behavior of one brain system influences other systems. Teacher-guides help students avoid neuronal confusion by thoughtfully involving all learning systems on the same task or encouraging noninvolved systems to remain neutral, rather than focusing on competing thoughts, feelings, or sensations.

For example, while developing knowledge about World War II *(cognitive learning system),* if students occasionally work in small groups *(social system)* to construct a replica of a concentration camp *(physical learning)* as a way of demonstrating how their great-grandparents *(personal relevance for emotional learning)* might have survived the Holocaust *(reflective learning),* then all five systems—or theaters of the mind—are actively attending to the same content.

This example gives an idea of how channeling the energy of each learning system on the same task can increase student engagement. Then, if the teacher-guide stimulates discussion about the coordinated process and asks students to contribute ideas for developing all systems while studying the next topic, he is fostering teacher/student collaboration while instilling the power of reflective thought.

Students who overreflect or overanalyze situations may assume blame for things not their fault. They may display high levels of anxiety or become depressed. These students need guidance for analysis of the past that leads to positive anticipated behavior for the future. In contrast, students who fail to exercise their reflective learning systems also may fail to take responsibility for past transgressions; as a result, they make few connections between today's behavior and future consequences. They tend to live in the here-and-now with no regard for the past or the future. Consequently, mild to severe conduct disorders may result. Clearly, guiding the reflective learning system's development is essential. Without attention to the extended consciousness that allows humans to think about their own thinking and do something about it, students could suffer severely.

Generally, the school curriculum omits direct instruction in purposeful reflection except in some programs that teach higher-order thinking skills. Yet, reflective learning is so important that it needs to be a part of all aspects of the curriculum. Teacher-guides ask questions like these:

➤ What worked, and what didn't?
➤ Why do you think that is so?
➤ How might your group design the next project differently so it works better?

As educators, we must allot time within lessons for reflective thought.

Thinking about one's own thinking can help reduce the human tendency to juggle too many mental balls at any one time. Also, careful planning to engage the five systems of the brain in a focused manner increases learning, whereas limited synchronization of the systems is like watching five different movies at the same time in the theaters of the mind.

To foster mastery of reflective learning, Perkins (1995) suggests that teachers emphasize the following:

➤ Strategies relevant to broad thinking challenges, such as remembering, problem solving, and decision making.
➤ Mental self-monitoring and management.
➤ Cultivation of positive attitudes.

To keep reminding ourselves of why we teach students to be reflective: "It seems that those who take the trouble to gain mastery over what happens in consciousness do live a happier life" (Csikszentmihalyi, 1990, p. 23). How we accomplish these tasks depends on how well we internalize a manageable framework, using all five learning systems, for instructional planning. Integrating the systems or theaters of the mind is the focus of the next chapter.

7

Theaters of the Mind

Various brain modules process information in parallel fashion throughout each hemisphere and from one hemisphere to the other, not in a step-by-step or serial fashion but—for the most part—simultaneously. For example, imagine sitting in a sunroom on a cool, crisp, bright day, reading a book. Even though your visual system is focused on printed symbols and their meaning, it also processes aspects of the sun's rays reflecting off the crystal pendent swinging in the window. Meanwhile, your auditory system is aware of the neighbor's son bouncing a basketball in the driveway. Smells of new-mown grass penetrate your olfactory system, and feelings in your lower abdomen prompt you to take a toilet break. Each system—and its multiple subsystems—functions like its own minitheater with its own internal movie playing. Thus, information processing resembles a multiplex movie theater where the brain's "theaters" never totally close, but remain ever vigilant in some wide-awake or sleepy state (Figure 7.1).

When input from the five major theaters simultaneously stimulates the brain's multimodal association areas, focused attention and learning occur. Confused thinking reigns, however, when the different systems attend to different "movies." This condition supports Edward de Bono's (1985) contention that the main difficulty of thinking is confusion. According to his research, people try to do too much at once and need to slow down their thinking and focus. That is what we do when we attend primarily to one mental movie or system and its subsystems; however, sounds, sights, and smells from the other systems intrude to demand equal attention like freshly popped corn beckoning us to the lobby. For example, intentions to revise a science report (cognitive system) can conflict with feeling the sting of a

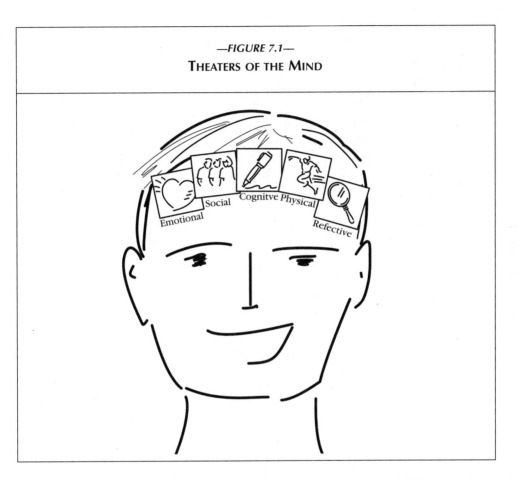

—*FIGURE 7.1*—
THEATERS OF THE MIND

teacher's sarcasm (emotional system), peer isolation when excluded from a group project (social system), discomfort of a racing heart (physical system), and anxiety at causing parental discord (reflective system). They are all like competing mind movies demanding equal attention.

The emotional, social, and physical learning systems tend to be the most powerful in terms of their demands. The level of their functioning determines how effectively the cognitive and reflective systems operate. Thus, even in the multiplex theaters of the mind, some movies overpower others. Figures 7.2 and 7.3 show how a lack of balance among the brain's natural learning systems negatively affects an individual when any one system either develops at the expense of others or becomes neglected.

—*FIGURE 7.2*—

PERSONAL EFFECTS OF OVERRELIANCE ON ONE LEARNING SYSTEM

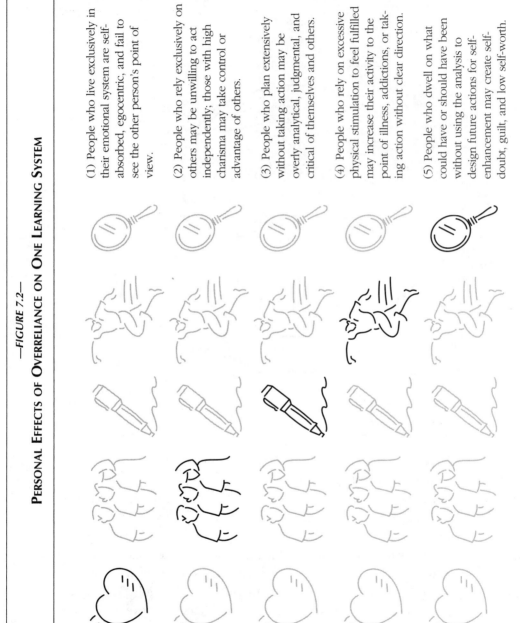

(1) People who live exclusively in their emotional system are self-absorbed, egocentric, and fail to see the other person's point of view.

(2) People who rely exclusively on others may be unwilling to act independently; those with high charisma may take control or advantage of others.

(3) People who plan extensively without taking action may be overly analytical, judgmental, and critical of themselves and others.

(4) People who rely on excessive physical stimulation to feel fulfilled may increase their activity to the point of illness, addictions, or taking action without clear direction.

(5) People who dwell on what could have or should have been without using the analysis to design future actions for self-enhancement may create self-doubt, guilt, and low self-worth.

—FIGURE 7.3—

PERSONAL EFFECTS WHEN A SYSTEM IS UNDERDEVELOPED

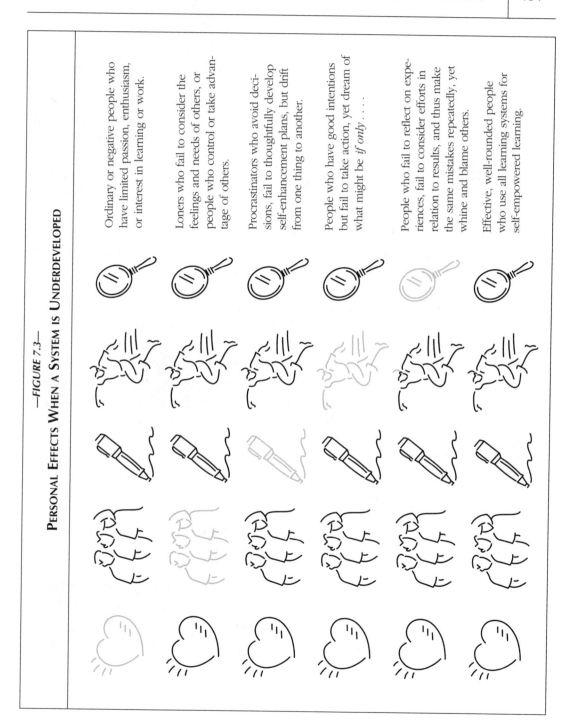

Ordinary or negative people who have limited passion, enthusiasm, or interest in learning or work.

Loners who fail to consider the feelings and needs of others, or people who control or take advantage of others.

Procrastinators who avoid decisions, fail to thoughtfully develop self-enhancement plans, but drift from one thing to another.

People who have good intentions but fail to take action, yet dream of what might be *if only . . . . .*

People who fail to reflect on experiences, fail to consider efforts in relation to results, and thus make the same mistakes repeatedly, yet whine and blame others.

Effective, well-rounded people who use all learning systems for self-empowered learning.

Multiply the theaters of one person's mind by the number of students and adults in a classroom, and try to imagine the mental complexities involved. It is staggering! Nonetheless, the five functional operating systems serve as a framework for teaching and learning to reduce the overall complexities. We can meet basic psychological needs collectively within a respectful learning environment and honor the individual learning systems within the classroom culture.

If teachers develop lesson plans and interact with students by consciously—and daily—addressing the brain's major learning systems or theaters of the mind, then schools can be a place where students are eager to go and reluctant to leave. By attending to each of the brain's natural learning systems, teachers and students can develop learning communities with a code of conduct where everyone expects and values achievement, where active learning is the standard. These are classrooms that promote friendships, where students desire group membership, and where each individual strives to achieve her personal best in the pursuit of personal learning goals. Although these standards are idealistic, our extended consciousness allows us to transform these imagined standards into today's classrooms. Why should teachers expect anything less of themselves and their students than to image the best? We must *see what we desire* in our mind's eye so we can convert what we imagine into reality. As an unknown poet once wrote: "You must give birth to your images, for they are future waiting to be born."

Teachers

Most people use the term *teacher*, which comes from Middle English, to mean "one who professes or imparts knowledge or skill." Before we understood that learning involves more than the intake of information, "professing" seemed quite adequate. But today, learning as a process is more akin to socialization than instruction, and it requires teachers who orchestrate development of the major learning systems within and across individuals (Ford, 1992).

Throughout this book, I introduced different teacher roles that support each of the learning systems: (1) model and mentor, (2) collaborator, (3) facilitator, (4) coach, and (5) talent scout and guide. Nowhere did I recommend the *lecturer* or *professor* role. Although content-oriented minilectures are sometimes appropriate, they should be kept short (10 minutes) or at least interspersed with meaningful student involvement.

If we rethink the term *teacher* as that of model and mentor, collaborator, facilitator, coach, and guide, the descriptions would cast a new light on how teachers view themselves and how they teach students. The process of teaching would focus on forming habits for lifelong learning, rather than just acquiring discrete fragments of information. But student development of agile learning habits throughout the brain's natural learning systems and teachers shifting from "professing" to more productive roles take concerted effort and time. As Wildman and Niles (1987) point out:

> Research on human learning implies that professional growth in teaching has an emerging quality, that the process takes substantial time, and that complex understandings and skills follow developmental patterns that have been understood in psychology for years but rarely applied to the training of teachers. . . . Complex understandings must be constructed from experience, and because experience can be constructed and reconstructed in many ways, the process is rarely ever finished. (pp. 5–6)

A rose by any other name is still a rose, but rethinking the concept of teaching dramatically alters what happens in the classroom and, consequently, what happens outside of it.

Learning Systems Summary

Just as we possess interconnected physical systems, we also maintain five interconnected learning systems associated with emotions, relationships, cognition, the senses, and assessment of self in one's environment.

Emotions

In brief, the emotional system determines personal passions, dreams, and desires. It projects a person's spirit, demeanor, and creativity, generating a sense of self that empowers and energizes or depresses and stifles all other systems. Emotional learning can be conscious, but it is generally unintentional or unconscious. For example, emotion—especially emotion occurring during critical periods of growth—programs specific reactions in a small almond-sized part of the brain called the amygdala. At the sight of a particular teacher who looks like someone who caused pain or injury in the past, the amygdala triggers physical reactions like anger, and the student feels uncomfortable but does not know why (Alkon, 1992). Emotional learning can also be deliberate, such as when convincing yourself to be genuinely happy for a friend who got the job you wanted.

Relationships

Social learning can also be either automatic or intentional. For instance, toddlers learn a language or develop prejudices and beliefs from family members automatically or without conscious effort. When peers work together to solve a problem, social learning becomes intentional and collaborative.

With the help of relationships, the social system governs interactions and communications with the self and others. It dictates what language develops, fosters collaborative problem solving, and honors individual diversity. The social system thrives on acceptance, love, and belonging.

Cognition

The cognitive system interprets, stores, and retrieves information; deliberately focuses on information; and intentionally provides input for all other systems. This system functions best when a person feels safe and secure rather than threatened. Cognitive learning is generally explicit—that is, intentional and purposeful (like much "school" learning)—however, it is also subject to implicit input from other systems.

For example, even though you may go to the library and research various car models and decide which one to purchase based on the model's maintenance record and gas mileage, a car salesman may say something to convince you differently by tapping into your emotional or social systems. While showing you a car of lower standards, for example, he may say, "I can see you are a lot like me; you are thoughtful and deliberate in your purchases. That makes my job of selling you this car much easier."

The implicit desired response is, "This salesman really respects me. He wouldn't sell me a car with lower standards than I desire." Thus, although your cognitive intent is to purchase based only on researched qualities, the salesman's expertise at triggering your emotional and social systems may result in a purchase you later regret (Cialdini, 1984).

The Senses

The physical system gathers information through the senses and distributes it throughout the brain and body. Responsible for converting input from all sensory and internal systems into action, this system functions best when the environment allows people to maintain control over personal actions and outcomes. Physical learning may take a long time to accomplish, such as when learning to ride a bicycle, but once learned, you can jump on one and ride down the street after years away from the trusty two-wheeler. In addition, physical learning can be reactive like the other systems. For example, children who grow up with lots of hugs tend to become *automatic* huggers. Those who grow up with physical abuse tend to become abusive.

The Self

The previous four systems—emotional, social, cognitive, and physical—operate within an environmental context to provide verbal and nonverbal learning opportunities for reflective learning. Because factors within specific environments and different circumstances vary, the reflective learning system acts as an ongoing monitoring mechanism for the individual. Reflective learning can be purposeful or automatic, unintentional, and unconscious. It is purposeful when the individual reflects: "Under these circumstances, in this environment, how am I doing? What do I need to do to increase my learning?"

Reflective learning weighs past, present, and probable thoughts and behaviors, and then predicts future outcomes by asking self-directed questions. This monitoring system plays a key role in determining how people function in society and how they construct their lives. It is automatic when elements or events in the environment influence learning without one's awareness; reactions occur without thought as to why or what to do about them. I once heard an inspirational speaker say that most people are *unconscious* most of the time, because they move through their days and nights on automatic pilot based on previously learned behavior. Bringing those kinds of behaviors to one's awareness and reflecting on them is part of the reflective learning system's function.

Learning systems are dynamical. They are active. They are constantly adjusting and adapting. And once adjusted, the new learning is irreversible. There is no way to go back and unlearn something. The learning may be forgotten, but it cannot be unlearned. Try unlearning how to tie a shoe or unlearn that President John F. Kennedy was shot in Dallas. It can't be done; thus learning systems are qualitatively and quantitatively different as a result of experience.

Educational Considerations

Educators can address the interplay among the learning systems by using them as a mental framework for planning lessons and instruction. Figure 7.4 provides a visual

—FIGURE 7.4—
Educational Implications of the Brain's Natural Learning Systems

The Brain's Natural Learning Systems	Learning Goal	Basic Learning Needs	Driving Behavior	Self-Directed Questions	Healthy Development of This System	Desired Teacher Behavior	Result of Over-reliance on This System	Result of Under-development of This System
Emotional	Self-direction	Need to be me	Passion	*Are my hopes, dreams, and desires for my highest good?*	**Self-Empowered Learning:** Develops a passion for achieving personal goals	Mentor model	**Self-absorbed.** Egocentric, selfish	**Slug.** Lethargic; lacks self-direction & motivation. Acts helpless
Social	Self-assurance	Need to belong	Vision and Collaboration	*Is my vision clear and socially responsible?*	**Collaborative Learning:** Interacts with others to develop a clear vision of goal attainment	Collaborator	**Overly Dependent.** Limited leadership skills or unhealthy control of others	**Isolate.** Fails to consider emotions & needs of others; antisocial.
Cognitive	Self-regulation	Need to know	Intention	*What knowledge and skills do I need? Am I planning effectively?*	**Strategic Learning:** Identifies needed knowledge and skills for goal attainment and develops plans for achieving them	Facilitator	**Fault-Finding.** Overly analytic; sees own approaches as only correct ones; nit-picks at others	**Aimless Drifter.** Procrastinates; develops limited knowledge & skills; avoids decisions.
Physical	Self-control	Need to do	Action	*Am I implementing my plan?*	**Active Learning:** Takes healthy action for goal attainment and self-systems management	Coach	**Physically Absorbed.** Excessive dependence on physical stimulation	**Dreamer.** Takes limited action toward goal attainment.
Reflective	Self-assessment	Need to experiment & explore	Reflection	*Am I making steady progress toward my goals? Do my actions match my values?*	**Reflective Learning:** Self-analyzes actions, attitudes, and accomplishments followed by predicting and anticipating the future	Talent Scout Guide	**Self-doubting.** Filled with guilt; dwells on own "mistakes"; fails to use them for continued progress	**Whiner.** Blames others for own failings.

representation of possible implications of the learning systems and how educators can use them to guide their own teaching and students' learning development.

Lesson plan development begins by determining what students need to know or be able to do (cognitive system). A board of education often makes this decision, which becomes articulated in the local or state standards of learning that identify the desired knowledge and skills. In other words, the standards build the foundation for evaluating knowledge and skill development. The next step is to brainstorm numerous ways to do the following:

1. Tap into students' personal goals and make the lessons personally relevant (emotional learning system).

2. Provide authentic solo, tandem, small-group, and teacher/student learning experiences that promote acceptance of diversity and generate a sense of belonging (social learning system).

3. Facilitate intentional learning for knowledge and skill construction through authentic problem-solving challenges (cognitive learning system).

4. Create active involvement through meaningful projects (physical learning system).

5. Teach students to analyze their progress, consider ways to enhance it, and develop plans for continued growth (reflective learning system).

These plans create a *passion* for learning, a *vision* of what is possible through *collaboration*, and a deliberate plan of *intention* supported by consistent and meaningful *action* and *reflection*. They address students' *need to be* ("I gotta be me!"), *need to belong, need to know, need to do,* and *need to experience and explore.*

Once the brainstorming for each system is exhausted, keep the resultant lists in a safe place for later use with subsequent units. Determine how much time is available for each unit of study and begin dividing the information into time segments in terms of weeks. Once you determine which content you intend to teach each week of the unit, use the lists to determine what each day will include, then divide the days into time units, and—toward the end of planning—into minutes for each part of the lesson.

Usually, a human interest story, related riddle, short video, or some other enjoyable way to tap into what students already know helps them connect personally to the topic. This is a good way to begin a new study or review something in progress or completed.

Remember also that when you provide experiences to students, you need to allow them to engage each major learning system and sensory modality without forcing them to use one that feels unnatural and uncomfortable. When you make various experiences available to students, they may try alternative ways of learning once they see others enjoying the experience, thereby tapping into their preferred learning styles and experimenting with other styles (Dunn & Dunn, 1992, 1993).

For example, material for students to read may be:

- tape recorded for those who prefer listening to the information,
- blocked into segments for tandem reading for those who work best with another person,
- presented with a list of questions for those who like focused reading,
- entered into a computer-driven program that highlights the text as it pronounces the words (such as with the Kurtzwell 3000 program),
- read within a small group where it can be discussed.

In a conference presentation, Marie Carbo, a reading specialist and learning-styles advocate, suggested that students who like to move may read while peddling a stationary bicycle with the book resting on a handlebar shelf. Rita and Kenneth Dunn (1992) suggest that children may be allowed to stand, walk, sway, sit, or lie on the floor while reading. The major stipulation of developing a learning-styles classroom is that students may use a specific accommodation if it does not interfere with the learning of others and if the student's performance is as good as or better than previous performance.

This brief overview of lesson development assumes that teachers reading this book have a basic pedagogical knowledge from which to draw. That background should be enough to experiment with teaching to the brain's natural learning systems. Without question, however, developing new teaching skills will take work, enthusiasm, and a determination to grow in one's chosen profession.

Summary

Three themes flow through this book. The first pertains to the brain-body's neurobiological operating systems for emotions, social interactions, cognitive functioning, physiological learning, and reflective insights. The second deals with environmental influences on those same systems; the third refers to the self-constructive nature of thinking and learning that controls and manipulates emotions, interactions, cognitions, behaviors, and reflective thought. From a rich mix of these three themes, I identify five major learning systems—emotional, social, cognitive, physical, and reflective—that can be used extensively as a framework for curriculum design and generic lesson planning, as well as a precursor for teaching to individual learning styles.

Because we, as humans, have five functional learning systems operating in specialized but parallel ways, we can mold ourselves into totally different human beings. We are not only conscious of things via our cognitive system, but also conscious of how we feel about them; therefore, it is reasonable to assume that we have a modular system concerned with emotion that is parallel to our cognitive system (Restak, 1994). By the same token, we are conscious of our culture and our preferences for working with partners and colleagues; we also know when we want to work alone. We are conscious of being active and engaged learners, and we know when we are passive and uninvolved in the learning process. We reflect on our past experiences and plan for the future. We develop strategies to help us learn, and we think about our own thinking. We do all these things while our natural learning systems address basic psychological needs unique to the human mind. When those needs are met, the systems function effectively. When our basic psychological needs go unmet, one or more of the systems are less than effective. Teachers can attend to the mind's psychological needs when they know what roles to play and what needs to address.

The neurobiological systems function in parallel like five theaters of the mind—all vying for attention. Teachers must respond in some meaningful and individually determined way to each of them. Not only must they accomplish this amazing feat for themselves, but they must also help students put their own learning systems together in personally satisfying, socially appropriate configurations. In other words, educators are in the business of brain construction: How we develop and implement lesson plans will determine—in large measure—what kinds of minds our students construct. The key to effective brain construction may be how teachers use the natural learning systems as a framework for linking neuroscience and education.

Glossary

acetylcholine. A highly pervasive neurotransmitter found in the brain, spinal cord, and ganglia—especially in centers controlling conscious movement. It operates all voluntary muscles and many involuntary muscles; it is the primary neurotransmitter for the autonomic nervous system; it mediates synaptic activity, is usually excitatory, and facilitates information processing with specific involvement in learning and memory circuits (Sylwester, 1995, p. 157).

adrenaline. Produced by the adrenal glands located on top of the kidneys, adrenaline—sometimes referred to as epinephrine—is controlled by sympathetic nerve fibers that also trigger the production of norepinephrine. Sympathetic nerve fibers are part of the visceral motor system that link emotions with physical reactions (Carlson, 1995; Purves et al., 2001). "Adrenaline release is a graded response dependent on the level of threat to the system" (Hannaford, 1995, p. 162).

alkaloid. Compound of vegetable origin that can be synthesized in solid or liquid form; can combine with acids; usually has pharmacological action, such as nicotine, morphine, or quinine.

amphetamine. "A synthetically produced central nervous system stimulant with cocaine-like effects; drug abuse may lead to dependence" (Purves et al., 2001, p. G-1).

amygdala. Located in the base of the temporal lobe, the amygdala is part of the limbic system and is involved in autonomic, emotional, and sexual behavior. It is formed by a nucleus or cluster of cell bodies that store memories of emotional events.

basal ganglia. "A group of nuclei [clusters of cell bodies] lying deep in the sub-cortical white matter of the frontal lobes that organize motor behavior" (Purves et al., 2001, p. G2).

brain stem. "The portion of the brain that lies between the diencephalon [thalamus and hypothalamus] and the spinal cord; comprises the midbrain, pons, and medulla" (Purves et al., 2001, p. G2).

Broca's area. "An area in the left frontal lobe specialized for the production of language" (Purves et al., 2001, p. G2).

catecholamines. Biologically active amino acids that include dopamine, norepinephrine, and epinephrine neurotransmitters; help produce alertness.

cerebellum. The prominent hindbrain structure composed of a three-layered cortex and deep nuclei. It plays a major role for motor coordination, posture, balance, and in integrating, sequencing, and smoothing movements (Carlson, 1995; Purves et al., 2001).

cingulate cortex. Semicircular structures just above the corpus callosum that wrap around the mid portion of the brain known as the limbic area.

corpus callosum. Bundle of axons that connect the two cerebral hemispheres of the brain so both sides of the brain can share electrochemical messages with each other.

corticotrophin-releasing factor (CRF). "A hypothalamic hormone that stimulates the anterior pituitary gland to secrete adrenocorticotrophic hormone (ACTH) which stimulates the adrenal cortex to produce various steroid hormones" (Carlson, 1995, p. 484).

cortisol. One of a group of glucocorticoids secreted by the adrenal glands when under stress. Cortisol (hydrocortisone) is the most abundant of these hormones; it increases blood sugar levels to provide needed energy in response to threat; "increased cortisol correlated with decreased learning and memory as well as attention problems" (Hannaford, 1995, p. 162).

dopamine. A catecholamine neurotransmitter that plays a role in the control of movements. For example, "Ritalin is thought to activate increased dopamine production within the brain, causing a decrease in hyperactive movement" (Hannaford, 1995, p. 200).

electroboard. An instructional tool with questions wired to answers; when question and answer are connected by a battery-powered continuity tester, the small bulb lights. This is a self-correcting tool for self-study.

electroencephalogram (EEG). A graphic record of minute changes in electric potential associated with the activity of the cerebral cortex, as detected by electrodes applied to the surface of the scalp to pick up signals that are sent to a computer for storage, review, and analysis.

electron microscopy. The use of a high-powered microscope to view electrons—the smallest particle of negative electricity.

endorphin. One of a group of neuropeptides (chain of amino acids), which serve as neurotransmitters, neuromodulators, or hormones. Endorphin is found naturally in, is endogenous to, the brain.

enkephalin. See the definition for endorphin.

enzyme. "A protein that facilitates a biochemical reaction without itself becoming part of the end product" (Carlson, 1995, p. 489).

flip chute. An instructional tool created from a milk or juice carton that allows a small card with a question on one side to be entered in a slit toward the top of the carton that exits from another slit toward the bottom. A chute inside the carton flips over the card so the answer side is shown when it exits. This tool provides a hands-on, self-correcting way for students to study questions and answers.

frontal cortex. The front portion of the cerebral cortex that includes Broca's speech area and the motor cortex, which spans across the top of the head.

ganglia. "Collections of hundreds of thousands of neurons found outside the brain and spinal cord along the course of peripheral nerves" (Purves et al., 2001, p. G5).

glial cells. Cells that support neurons in the central nervous system; their functions are not altogether clear.

hippocampus. "A cortical structure in the medial portion of the temporal lobe; in humans, concerned with short-term declarative memory, among many other functions" (Purves et al., p. G6).

hypothalamus. A collection of small but critical clusters of cell bodies (nuclei) lying inferior to the thalamus; "governs reproductive, homeostatic, and circadian functions" (Purves et al., 2001, p. G6).

kinesthetic. Pertaining to motion; characterized by movement. A kinesthetic learner likes authentic experiences and active involvement in the learning process.

learning system. Neuronal modules, circuits, and pathways that link together for processing similar input; they are subject to modification based on environmental stimulation.

limbic area. Cortical and subcortical structures concerned with emotions; includes the cingulate gyrus, hippocampus, and amygdala.

methylphenidate. Scientific name for Ritalin, a drug prescribed for hyperactivity.

midbrain. Portion of the brain immediately above the brain stem that controls automatic (reflex) patterns of the visual and auditory sensory systems.

module. Clusters or "islands of gray matter" composed of "thousands if not millions of neurons" that, "at any given moment," are altering their connections with each other to create "multiple connections all operating simultaneously and in parallel" to construct what we see, feel, create, remember, think, visualize, and so forth (Restak, 1994, pp. xvii & 5).

modular brain. Horizontal and vertical neuronal patterns of neurons that cluster into "columns" or "modules" that respond in some behavioral way to specific stimuli, in a connected way with "all other parts of the brain" (Restak, 1994, p. 33). Modular "function resides in different brain areas at different times depending on the circumstances. . . . The brain operates as a complex of reciprocally interconnected systems" (p. 34). "The brain is arranged according to a distributed system composed of large numbers of modular elements linked together. That means the information flow through such a system may follow a number of different pathways, and the dominance of one path or another is a dynamic and changing property of the system" (Mountcastle, cited in Restak, 1994, p. 35).

neocortex. The phylogenetically newest part of the brain that includes primary sensory, motor, and association areas or cortices.

neurobiology. The study of anatomical and physiological neural networks and mechanisms in an attempt to decipher how the brain functions.

neuron. Brain cell specialized for conducting and transmitting electrochemical signals in the nervous system.

neurotransmitter. Chemical substance released at the axon terminals of one brain cell and transmitted across the synaptic gap to other brain cells.

norepinephrine. A neurotransmitter that "enhances blood flow to skeletal muscles and increases heart and respiratory rates, blood pressure, and the blood sugar level, providing a mechanism for stress reactions" (Diamond et al., 1985, p. 8-1).

nucleus accumbens. A cluster of cell bodies that receives dopamine secretions; thought to be involved in reinforcement and attention (Purves et al., 2001, p. G-10).

opioid. "Any natural or synthetic drug that has pharmacological actions similar to those of morphine" (Purves et al., 2001, p. G-10).

oxytocin. A brain chemical involved with social processes such as female sex, orgasm, maternal behavior, and social memory; deals with birthing and milk let-down, maternal acceptance and readiness (Panksepp, 1998, pp. 101–102).

peptide. "A chain of amino acids joined by peptide bonds. Many peptides produced by cells of the brain serve as neurotransmitters, neuromodulators, or hormones. Proteins are long peptides" (Carlson, 1995, p. 495).

periaqueductal gray (PAG). "Region of brainstem gray matter that contains, among others, nuclei associated with the modulation of pain perception" (Purves et al., 2001, p. G11).

plasticity. "Term that refers to structural or functional changes in the nervous system" (Purves et al., 2001, p. G11).

potentiation. A dendrite and neuron that are repeatedly stimulated increase the supply of neurotransmitters for information transmission; dendrites become more complex by increasing the receptor surface to take advantage of the increased amount of neurotransmitter available (Joseph, 1993, p. 340).

prefrontal cortex. "Cortical regions in the frontal lobe that are anterior to the primary and association motor cortices; thought to be involved in planning complex cognitive behaviors and in the expression of personality and appropriate social behavior" (Purves et al., 2001, p. G11).

serotonin. "A biogenic amine neurotransmitter derived from the amino acid tryptophan" (Purves et al., 2001, p. G-13).

sociopath. An antisocial personality disorder sometimes referred to as a psychopathy characterized as follows: "Incapable of remorse and slow to learn from their mistakes, the antisocial flaunt an open disregard for the rights of others" (Niehoff, 1999, p. 129).

synapse. Release of a chemical transmitter from the axonal terminal of one neuron and the reception of that chemical by another.

task cards. Cards—often hand-held—that have questions on one side or portion and answers on the other.

thalamus. A walnut-sized cluster of neurons with many sections that receive information from and send information to the cerebral cortex; often called the brain's gatekeeper.

tryptophan. An amino acid; the precursor for serotonin.

tyrosine. An amino acid; the precursor of dopamine, norepinephrine, and epinephrine—all catecholamines.

vestibular system. A system of neurons within the inner ear that includes a nodule on the vestibular nerve and two receptor sacs or organs that detect changes in the tilt of the head and convey information to the brain.

Wernicke's Area. "A region of auditory cortex on the left temporal lobe of humans, which is important in the comprehension of words and the production of meaningful speech. Wernicke's aphasia, which occurs as a result of damage to this area, results in fluent but meaningless speech" (Carlson, 1995, p. 501).

Zone of Proximal Development. The level of task difficulty that is neither too difficult nor too easy, but comfortably challenging within one's grasp; term coined by Lev Vygotsky in 1962 (see Vygotsky, 1978).

References

Ackerman, D. (1990). *A natural history of the senses.* New York: Vintage Books.

Alkon, D. L. (1992). *Memory's voice: Deciphering the mind-brain code.* New York: Harper Collins.

Amen, D. G. (1995). *Windows into the A.D.D. mind: Understanding and treating attention deficit disorders in the everyday lives of children, adolescents, and adults.* Fairfield, CA: MindWorks Press.

Andrews, R. H. (1990). The development of a learning styles program in a low socioeconomic, underachieving North Carolina elementary school. *Journal of Reading, Writing, and Learning Disabilities International, 6,* 307–314.

Baars, B. (1997). *Theaters of consciousness: The workplace of the mind.* New York: Oxford University Press.

Barkley, R. A. (2000). *Taking charge of ADHD: The complete, authoritative guide for parents.* New York: Guilford Press.

Benedict, R. (1934). *Patterns of culture.* Boston: Houghton Mifflin.

Bentov, I. (1977/1988). *Stalking the wild pendulum: On the mechanics of consciousness.* Rochester, VT: Destiny Books.

Berreth, D., & Scherer, M. (1993, November). On transmitting values: A conversation with Amitai Etzioni. *Educational Leadership, 51*(3), 12–15.

Blackmore, S. (1999). *The meme machine.* New York: Oxford University Press.

Borich, G. D., & Tombari, M. L. (1997). *Educational psychology: A contemporary approach* (2nd ed.). New York: Longman.

Brothers, L. (1997). *Friday's footprint: How society shapes the human mind.* New York: Oxford University Press.

Bruer, J. (1998, November). Brain science, brain fiction. *Educational Leadership, 56*(3), 14–18.

Bruer, J. (1999, December). Neural connections: Some you use, some you lose. *Phi Delta Kappan,* 81(4), 264–277.

Campbell, D. (1997). *The Mozart effect: Tapping the power of music to heal the body, strengthen the mind, and unlock the creative spirit.* New York: Avon Books.

Carlson, N. R. (1995). *Foundations of physiological psychology* (3rd ed.). Needham Heights, MA: Simon & Schuster.

Cialdini, R. B. (1984). *Influence: How and why people agree to things.* New York: Quill.

Coloroso, B. (1990). *Winning at teaching . . . without beating your kids* (Cassette and video recordings). Littleton, CO: Kids Are Worth It! Inc.

Conners, C. K. (1989). *Feeding the brain: How foods affect children.* Reading, MA: Perseus Books.

Covey, S. R. (1989). *The seven habits of highly effective people: Restoring the character ethic.* New York: A Fireside Book/Simon and Schuster.

Crick, F. (1994). *The astonishing hypothesis: The scientific search for the soul.* New York: Scribner.

Csikszentmihalyi, M. (1990). *Flow: The psychology of optimal experience.* New York: Harper Perennial, HarperCollins.

Csikszentmihalyi, M. (1993). *The evolving self: A psychology for the third millennium.* New York: HarperCollins.

Damasio, A. (1994). *Descartes' error: Emotion, reason, and the human brain.* New York: A Grosset/Putnam Book.

Damasio, A. (1999). *The feeling of what happens: Body and emotion in the making of consciousness.* New York: Harcourt Brace.

Damasio, A. (2000, November 23) Inside the theatre of the mind. [Online article]. *Electronic Telegraph.* Available: http://www.telegraph.co.uk. Search Damasio.

Dawkins, R. (1976/1989). *The selfish gene.* New York: Oxford University Press.

De Bono, E. (1969/1985). *The mechanism of mind.* New York: Penguin Books.

Dehaene, S. (1997). *The number sense: How the mind creates mathematics.* New York: Oxford University Press.

Denham, S. A. (1998). *Emotional development in young children.* New York: Guilford Press.

Dennison, P. E., & Dennison, G. E. (1994). *Brain gym* (Teacher's ed., rev.). Ventura, CA: Edu-Kinesthetics.

Deshler, D., & Schumaker, B. J. (1988). An instructional model for teaching students how to learn. In J. Graden, J. Zins, & M. Curtis (Eds.), *Alternative educational delivery systems: Enhancing instructional options for all students* (pp. 391–411). Washington, DC: National Association of School Psychologists.

Diamond, M. C. (1988). *Enriching heredity: The impact of the environment on the anatomy of the brain.* New York: The Free Press.

Diamond, M., & Hopson, J. (1998). *Magic trees of the mind: How to nurture your child's intelligence, creativity, and healthy emotions from birth through adolescence.* New York: A Dutton Book, Penguin Putnam.

DiIulio, Jr., J. (1994, Spring/Summer). America's ticking crime bomb and how to defuse it. *Wisconsin Interest, 3*(1). (Milwaukee, WI: Wisconsin Policy Research Institute, Inc.).

Donald, M. (1991). *Origins of the modern mind.* Cambridge, MA: Harvard University Press.

Dozier, R. W., Jr. (1998). *Fear itself: The origin and nature of the powerful emotion that shapes our lives and our world.* New York: St. Martin's Press.

Dunn, R., & Dunn, K. (1992). *Teaching young children through their individual learning styles: Practical approaches for grades K-2.* Boston: Allyn and Bacon.

Dunn, R., Griggs, S., Olson, I., Beasley, M., & Gorman, B. (1995). A meta-analytic validation of the Dunn and Dunn model of learning-style preferences. *The Journal of Educational Research, 88* (61), 353–362.

Edelman, G. M. (1992). *Bright air, brilliant fire: On the matter of the mind.* New York: Basic Books.

Eisenberg, D. (1993a). Another way of seeing. Interview with Bill Moyers in *Healing and the mind* (pp. 305–314). New York: Doubleday.

Eisenberg, D. (1993b). Medicine in mind/body culture. Interview with Bill Moyers in *Healing and the mind* (pp. 257–303). New York: Doubleday.

Elkind, D. (1978). *The child's reality: Three developmental themes.* Hillsdale, NJ: Lawrence Erlbaum.

Ellis, A. (1973). *Humanistic psychotherapy: The rational-emotive approach* (E. Sagarin, Ed.). New York: Julian Press.

Erikson, E. H. (1982). *The life cycle completed.* New York: Norton.

Felten, D. (1993). The brain and the immune system. Interview with Bill Moyers in *Healing and the mind* (pp. 213–237). New York: Doubleday.

Feurestein, R. (1980*). Instrumental enrichment: An intervention program for cognitive modifiability.* Baltimore: University Park Press.

Ford, M. E. (1992). *Motivating humans: Goals, emotions, and personal agency beliefs.* Newbury Park, CA: Sage.

Gardner, H. (1985). *Frames of mind: The theory of multiple intelligences.* New York: Basic Books.

Gardner, H., & Veins, J. (1990, Winter). Multiple intelligence and styles: Partners in effective education. *The Clearinghouse Bulletin* (pp. 4–5). Seattle, WA: Antioch University.

Gazzaniga, M. S. (1985). *The social brain: Discovering the networks of the mind.* New York: Basic Books.

Gazzaniga, M. S. (1992). *Nature's mind: The biological roots of thinking, emotions, sexuality, language, and intelligence.* New York: Basic Books.

Gazzaniga, M. S., Ivry, R. B., & Mangun, G. R. (1998). *Cognitive neuroscience: The biology of the mind.* New York: W. W. Horton & Co.

Giedd, J. N., Blumethal, J., Jeffries, N. O., Castellanos, F. X., Liu, H., Zijdenbos, A., Paus, T., Evans, A., & Rapoport, J. L. (1999, October). Brain development during childhood and adolescence: A longitudinal MRI study. *Nature Neuroscience, 2*(10), 861-863. . *Note:* May 2, 2000, comments made at The White House conference on teenagers: Raising responsible and resourceful youth. Washington, D. C.: White House Office of the Press Secretary may be found at http://clinton4.nara.gov/WH/New/html/20000420.html

Given, B. K. (1991). Integrated strategies instruction. In L. Korinek & J. Engelhard (Eds.), *Virginia presents: Best practices. Challenges for the nineties: Selected papers from the Council for Learning Disabilities 12th International Conference on Learning Disabilities* (pp. 26–32). Williamsburg, VA: College of William and Mary.

Given, B. K. (1994). Operation breakthrough for continuous self-systems improvement. *Intervention in School and Clinic, 30*(1), 38–46.

Given, B. K. (1997). Emotional learning: Getting back to the basics. *Wisconsin School News, 52*(5), 8–18.

Given, B. K. (1998, November). Food for thought. *Educational Leadership, 56*(8), 68–71.

Given, B. K. (2000). Theaters of the mind. *Educational Leadership, 58*(30), 72–75.

Goleman, D. (1995). *Emotional intelligence: Why it can matter more than IQ.* New York: Bantam Books.

Goerner, S. J. (1994). *Chaos and the evolving ecological universe.* Langhorne, PA: Gordon and Breach Science Publishers.

Greenfield, S. A. (Ed.) (1996). *The human mind explained.* New York: Henry Holt.

Greenfield, S. A. (1997). *The human brain: A guided tour.* New York: Basic Books.

Greenspan, S. I. (1997). *The growth of the mind: And the endangered origins of intelligence.* Reading, MA: Addison-Wesley.

Griffiths, P. E. (1997). *What emotions really are: The problem of psychological categories.* Chicago: University of Chicago Press.

Guenther, R. K. (1998). *Human cognition.* New Jersey: Prentice-Hall.

Halperin, J. M. (1996). Conceptualizing, describing, and measuring components of attention: A summary. In G. R. Lyon & N. Krasnegor (Eds.), *Attention, memory, and executive function* (pp. 57–69). Baltimore: Paul H. Brookes.

Hamer, D., & Copeland, P. (1998). *Living with our genes: Why they matter more than you think.* New York: Doubleday.

Hannaford, C. (1995). *Smart moves: Why learning is not all in your head.* Arlington, VA: Great Ocean Publishers.

Harris, J. R. (1998). *The nurture assumption: Why children turn out the way they do.* New York: The Free Press.

Hawkes, N. (2001, February 13). Nature beats nurture. *The Times* [Online]. Available: http://www.thetimes.co.uk/article/0,,7-82727.html.

Hebb, D. O. (1949). *Organization of behavior: A neuropsychological theory.* New York: Wiley.

Hecker, L. (1997, October). Walking, Tinkertoys, and Legos: Using movement and manipulatives to help students write. *English Journal, 86*(6), 46–52.

Hobson, J. A. (1994). *The chemistry of conscious states: How the brain changes its mind.* Boston: Little, Brown.

Howard, P. J. (1994). *The owner's manual for the brain.* Austin, TX: Bard.

Jackendoff, R. (1994). *Patterns in the mind: Language and human nature.* New York: Basic Books.

Johnson, D. J., & Myklebust, H. R. (1967). *Learning disabilities: Educational principles and practices.* New York: Grune & Stratton.

Jones, R. (1992). Ego identity and adolescent problem behavior. In G. Adams, T. Gullotta, & R. Montemayor (Eds.), *Adolescent identity formation* (pp. 216–233). Newbury Park, CA: Sage.

Jones, S. (1994). *The language of the genes: Biology, history and the evolutionary future.* Hammersmith, London: HarperCollins.

Joseph, R. (1993). *The naked neuron.* New York: Plenum Press.

Joseph, R. (1996). *Neuropsychiatry, neuropsychology, and clinical neuroscience* (2nd ed.). Baltimore: Williams & Wilkins.

Kagan, J. (1994). *Galen's prophecy: Temperament in human nature.* New York: Basic Books.

Kavale, K. A., Hirshoren, A., & Forness, S. R. (1998). Meta-analytic validation of the Dunn and Dunn model of learning-style preferences: A critique of what was Dunn. *Learning Disabilities Research and Practice, 13*(2), 75–80.

Kawasaki, H., Adolphs, R., Kaufman, O., Damasio, H., Damasio, A. R., Granner, M., Bakken, H., Hori, T., & Howard III, M. A. (2001). Single-neuron responses to emotional visual stimuli recorded in human ventral prefrontal cortex. *Nature Neuroscience, 4*(1), 15–16.

Kotulak, R. (1996). *Inside the brain: Revolutionary discoveries of how the mind works.* Kansas City, MO: Andrews & McMeel.

LeDoux, J. (1996). *The emotional brain: The mysterious underpinnings of emotional life.* New York: Simon & Schuster.

Lickona, T. (1993, November). The return of character education. *Educational Leadership, 51*(3), 6–11.

Linnoila, M., Virkkunen, M., Scheinin, M., Nuutila, A., Rimon, R., & Goodwin, F. K. (1994). Low cerebrospinal fluid 5-hydroxyindoleacetic acid concentration differentiates impulsive from nonimpulsive violent behavior. In R. Masters & M. McGuire (Eds.), *The neurotransmitter revolution: Serotonin, social behavior, and the law* (pp. 62–68). Carbondale, IL: Southern Illinois University Press.

Luria, A. R. (1973). *The working brain: An introduction to neuropsychology.* New York: Basic Books.

MacLean, P. (1990). *The triune brain in evolution.* New York: Plenum Press.

McMurry, J. (1984). *Essentials of general, organic, and biological chemistry.* Englewood Cliffs, NJ: Prentice Hall.

McNulty, P. (1995, Winter). Natural born killers? Preventing the coming explosion of teenage crime. *Policy Review, Nov.,* pp. 86–97. (Washington, DC: Heritage Foundation).

Milgram, R. M., Dunn, R., & Price, G. E. (1993). *Teaching and counseling gifted and talented adolescents: An international learning style perspective.* Westport, CT: Praeger.

Mills, J. C., & Crowley, R. J. (1986). *Therapeutic metaphors for children and the child within.* New York: Brunner/Mazel.

Mirsky, A. F. (1996). Disorders of attention: A neuropsychological perspective. In G. R. Lyon & N. Krasnegor (Eds.), *Attention, memory, and executive function* (pp. 57–69). Baltimore: Paul H. Brookes.

Moyers, B. (1993). *Healing and the mind.* New York: Doubleday.

National Center for Juvenile Justice. (2000). *Crime in the United States 1999.* [Online] Washington, DC: U. S. Government Printing Office. Available: http://www.ojjdp.ncjrs.org/ojstatbb/qa250.html.

Nesbit, J. (1994). *Global paradox: The bigger the world economy, the more powerful its smallest players.* New York: William Morrow.

Niehoff, D. (1999). *The biology of violence: How understanding the brain, behavior, and environment can break the vicious circle of aggression.* New York: The Free Press.

Obrzut, J. O., & Hynd, G. W. (Eds.) (1991). *Neuropsychological foundations of learning disabilities: A handbook of issues, methods, and practice.* New York: Academic Press.

Office of Juvenile Justice and Delinquency Prevention (OJJDP). (2000, December). *OJJDP statistical briefing book.* [Online]. Available: http://ojjdp.ncjrs.org/ojstatbb/.

Ornish, D. (1993). Changing life habits. In B. Moyers (Ed.), *Healing and the mind* (pp. 87–113). New York: Doubleday.

Ornstein, R. (1986). *Multimind: A new way of looking at human behavior.* New York: Anchor Books, Doubleday.

Orr, D. (2001, February 13). Good news: Life is what we make it. [Online]. *Independent Argument.* Available: http://www.independent.co.uk/argument/Regular_columnists/Deborah_Orr/orr130201.shtml. No longer available.

Panksepp, J. (1998). *Affective neuroscience: The foundations of human and animal emotions.* New York: Oxford University Press.

Perkins, D. (1995). *Outsmarting IQ: The emerging science of learnable intelligence.* New York: The Free Press.

Pert, C. B. (1993). Interview: The chemical communicators. In B. Moyers (Ed.), *Healing and the mind* (pp. 177–193). New York: Doubleday.

Pert, C. B. (1997). *Molecules of emotion. Why you feel the way you feel.* New York: Scribner.

Pinker, S. (1994). *The language instinct.* New York: William Morrow.

Pinker, S. (1997). *How the mind works.* New York: W. W. Norton.

Purves, D., Augustine, G. J., Fitzpatrick, D., Katz, L. C., LaMantia, A. S., McNamara, I. O., & Williams, S. M. (Eds.) (2001). *Neuroscience* (2nd ed.). Sunderland, MA: Sinaver Associates, Inc.

Rapp, D. (1996). *Is this your child's world? How you can fix the schools and homes that are making your children sick.* New York: Bantam Books.

Restak, R. M. (1991). *The brain has a mind of its own: Insights from a practicing neurologist.* New York: Crown Trade Paperbacks.

Restak, R. M. (1993/1994). *Receptors.* New York: Bantam Books.

Restak, R. M. (1994). *The modular brain: How new discoveries in neuroscience are answering age-old questions about memory, free will, consciousness, and personal identity.* New York: Charles Scribner's Sons.

Sapolsky, R. M. (1994). *Why zebras don't get ulcers: A guide to stress, stress-related diseases, and coping.* New York: W. H. Freeman.

Sergeant, J. (1996). A theory of attention: An information processing perspective. In G. R. Lyon & N. Krasnegor (Eds.), *Attention, memory, and executive function* (pp. 57–69). Baltimore: Paul H. Brookes.

Silver, H. F., Strong, R. W., and Perini, M. I. (2000). *So each may learn: Integrating learning styles and multiple intelligences.* Alexandria, VA: Association for Supervision and Curriculum Development.

Spreen, O., Risser, A., & Edgett, D. (1995). *Developmental neuropsychology.* New York: Oxford University Press.

Sprinthall, N. A., Sprinthall, R. C., & Oja, S. N. (1994). *Educational psychology: A developmental approach* (6th ed.). New York: McGraw-Hill.

Sternberg, E. M. (2000). *The balance within: The science connecting health and emotions.* New York: W. H. Freeman.

Stitt, B. R. (1997). *Food and behavior: A natural connection.* Manitowoc, WI: Natural Press.

Stone, P. (1992). How we turned around a problem school. *Principal, 71*(2), 34–36.

Stuss, D. & Benson F. (1992, June). "No longer gage": Frontal lobe dysfunction and emotional changes. *Journal of Consulting & Clinical Psychology, 60*(3), 349–359.

Sylwester, R. (1995). *A celebration of neurons: An educator's guide to the human brain.* Alexandria, VA: Association for Supervision and Curriculum Development.

Sylwester, R. (2000). *A biological brain in a cultural classroom: Applying biological research to classroom management.* Thousand Oaks, CA: Corwin Press.

Tice, D. M., Bratslavsky, E., & Baumeister, R. F. (2001). Emotional distress regulation takes precedence over impulse control: If you feel bad, do it! *Journal of Personality and Social Psychology, 80*(1), 53–67.

Ullian, E. M., Sapperstein, S. K., Christopherson, K. S., & Barres, B. A. (2001, January 26). Control of synapse number by glia. [Online]. *Science, 291*(5504), 569–570. Available: http://sciencemag.org. Search for Ullian.

U.S. Department of Justice. (1996). *Juvenile offenders and victims: 1996 update on violence.* [Online]. Washington, DC: Office of Juvenile Justice and Delinquency Prevention. U.S. Government Printing Office. Available: http://www.ncjrs.org/pdffiles/90995.pdf.

U.S. Department of Justice. (2001). *NCPA fact sheet on juvenile crime.* [Online]. Juvenile Justice Hotline. Available: http://www.ncpa.org/hotlines/juvcrm/eocp1.html.

Violence Institute of New Jersey. (2001). *School and youth violence statistics.* [Online]. Available: http://www.umdnj.edu/vinjweb/stats.html. Search VINJ Materials for statistics.

Vygotsky, L. (1978). *Mind in society.* Cambridge, MA: Harvard University Press.

Wagner, R. K. (1996). From simple structure to complex function: Major trends in the development of theories, models, and measurements of memory. In G. R. Lyon & N. Krasnegor (Eds.), *Attention, memory, and executive function* (pp. 57–69). Baltimore: Paul H. Brookes.

Wildman, T. M., & Niles, J. A. (1987, February). Essentials of professional growth. *Educational Leadership, 44*(5), 4–10.

Wilson, J. J. (2000, October). Offenders in juvenile court, 1997. [Online]. *Juvenile Justice Bulletin.* Available: http://www.ncjrs.org/html/ojjdp/jjbul2000_10_3/contents.html.

Wright, R. (1994). *The moral animal: Why we are the way we are: The new science of evolutionary psychology.* New York: Vintage Books.

Wurtman, J. J. (1988). *Managing your mind and mood through food.* New York: Harper & Row.

Wurtman, J. J., & Suffes, S. (1996/1997). *Serotonin solution.* New York: Fawcett Columbine.

Index

Note: an *f* after a page number indicates a figure.

About the Author

Barbara K. Given is the Director of the Adolescent Learning Research Center, Krasnow Institute for Advanced Studies, and an Associate Professor, Graduate School of Education at George Mason University in Fairfax, Virginia, where she initiated the Special Education Teacher Preparation Program. She has written several articles relating brain research to education; three of them were published by ASCD. She also wrote *Learning Styles: A Guide for Teachers and Parents*.

After completing an Associate of Arts degree from Colorado Woman's College in Denver, Barbara Given began her teaching career as an assistant teacher at Laradon Hall, a school for mentally retarded youngsters. She completed an elementary education undergraduate degree at Kansas State University, a Master of Science degree in elementary education at the University of Oregon, and a Ph.D. in education of the exceptional at The Catholic University of America. En route to these academic milestones, she taught 2nd grade and youngsters with mental retardation, learning disabilities, and emotional disturbances at different grade levels. She also served as the principal of the Kennedy Habilitation Center in Baltimore and as an adjunct professor at two universities before accepting an appointment at George Mason University. Given was twice honored as being one of the University's outstanding scholars. She also has two grown and married children, Bryce and Bethany.

Contact the author via e-mail (bgiven@gmu.edu), phone (703-993-4406), or fax (703-993-4325).

Related ASCD Resources: The Brain and Learning

ASCD stock numbers are in parentheses.

Audiotapes

Achieving Major Goals with Brain-Based Learning, by Joan Caulfield and Wayne Jennings (#200173)

Brains and Education: A Partnership for Life by Marian Diamond (#299231)

Emotion/Attention: Our Brain's Doorway to Reason and Logic by Robert Sylwester (#200114)

How Can Educators Use Knowledge About the Human Brain to Improve School Learning? by Eric Jensen, Renate Nummela Caine, and Robert Sylwester (#200096)

How the Young Brain Learns (3 tapes) by JoAnn Barney, Steve Petersen, and Andy Meltzoff (#200292)

Staff Development with the Brain in Mind by Eric Jensen (#200139)

Using Learning Styles, Multiple Intelligences, and Brain Research to Promote Student Literacy by Harvey F. Silver and Richard W. Strong (#201182)

Multimedia

The Human Brain Professional Inquiry Kit by Bonnie Benesh (#99900)

Networks

Visit the ASCD Web site (www.ascd.org) and search for "networks" for information about professional educators who have formed groups around topics like "Authentic Assessment," "Brain-Based Compatible Learning," and "Building Intrinsically Motivating Environments." Look in the "Network Directory" for current facilitators' addresses and phone numbers.

Online Resources

Visit ASCD's Web site (www.ascd.org) for the following professional development opportunities: *Educational Leadership: How the Brain Learns* (entire issue, November 1998). Excerpted articles online free (http://www.ascd.org/frameedlead.html); entire issue online and accessible to ASCD members (http://www.ascd.org/membersonly.html)

Online Tutorials: *The Brain and Learning, Constructivism,* and *Performance Assessments,* among others (http://www.ascd.org/frametutorials.html) (free)

Professional Development Online: *The Brain* and *Memory and Learning Strategies,* among others (http://www.ascd.org/framepdonline.html) (for a small fee; password protected)

Print Products

Arts with the Brain in Mind by Eric Jensen (#101011)

ASCD Topic Pack: *Brain-Based Learning Topic Pack* (#197194)

A Celebration of Neurons: An Educator's Guide to the Human Brain by Robert Sylwester (#195085)

Brain Matters: Translating Research into Classroom Practice by Patricia Wolfe (#101004)

Learning and Memory: The Brain in Action by Marilee Sprenger (#199213)

Teaching with the Brain in Mind by Eric Jensen (#198019)

Videotapes

The Brain and Early Childhood (two tapes, #400054)

The Brain and Learning (four tapes, #498062)

The Brain and Mathematics Series (two tapes, #400237)

The Brain and Reading (three tapes, #499207)

For additional information, visit us on the World Wide Web (http://www.ascd.org), send an e-mail message to member@ascd.org, call the ASCD Service Center (1-800-933-ASCD or 703-578-9600, then press 2), send a fax to 703-575-5400, or write to Information Services, ASCD, 1703 N. Beauregard St., Alexandria, VA 22311-1714 USA.